Leopard in the Kitchen
And Other Amazing Tales From East Africa

From the pages of Old Africa magazine

Copyright © 2013 Old Africa magazine
All rights reserved. No part of this text may be reproduced, photocopied or otherwise used in any way without the prior written approval and consent of Old Africa.

ISBN# 979-8681-9845-8-0

Published by Old Africa

A division of Kifaru Educational and Editorial Consultants LTD

PO Box 2338, Naivasha, 20117, Kenya

Printed in the Nairobi by English Press

Cover design and layout by Blake Arensen

The Wildlife of East Africa

Leopard in the Kitchen

I arrived in Kenya in 1956 and entered the colonial administration as Temporary District Officer during the Emergency. Early in 1957 I received instructions to meet the senior District Officer, David Worthy of Upper Abothoguthi, in the Meru district of Kenya, an area close under and east of Mount Kenya. After I unpacked at my station, Katheri Boma, I asked David Worthy with some trepidation, "What is my job?"

His reply has stuck with me ever since. "Out there," he said waving his hand vaguely at a view of distant hills, forests and scattered Africa villages, "there are about twenty thousand Africans and anything that concerns them concerns you."

From Katheri boma my next-door neighbour was the DO at Mitunguuguu in Lower Abothoguchi, Alec Shillinglaw, a Scotsman from deepest Glasgow who became a good friend.

The love of Alec's life was his dog, a vast mastiff of uncertain lineage and temperament widely known and respected by the Meru as sleeping o'nights on Alec's wide veranda. One tragic night a leopard came and carried away Alec's dog. The only sign left of the deed in the morning was the leopard's pugmarks. Alec's reaction moved rapidly from sorrow to anger to desire for revenge upon this dastardly carnivore. He set up a trap. Alongside his dwelling house he had a kitchen stoutly built of heavy vertical timbers not unlike his own quarters but with no window. He tethered a goat in the kitchen and left its stout timber door ajar but sprung to close upon entry. Alec was woken in the wee sma' hours by pandemonium in his kitchen: goat a-crying and leopard a-leaping. Alec's problem now was how to shoot the beast through a closed door and avoid the goat.

Using a Tribal Policeman's 12-bore shotgun (with SSG, extra large shot provided for anti-personnel use, rather than normal birdshot) Alec blasted away to rather little effect. Then he blasted off the door's lock and shot through the enlarged keyhole.

Eventually noise and movement from inside the kitchen slowed and Alec opened the door. A scene of absolute chaos confronted him. Hardly a cooking pot was left complete and quite an amount of broken china littered the floor. The leopard was dead, but unfortunately the goat was dying.

Neil McGlashan, Tasmania

Rhino Charges Land Rover!

We visited Ruaha National Park in the mid-1970s with our sons, Peter and David, then teenagers, and some friends from the Tanganyika Wattle Company in Njombe. We drove around in two Land Rovers towards the Mwayembe swamp area. The Land Rover driven by Dr 'Eck' Eckhart with his wife Donnie, and our two sons in it, led the way. Jobst and I and another friend, a keen photographer, were not far behind. We were driving slowly and the leading Land Rover stopped. There was a very peaceful, lovely scene of some zebra, impala and giraffe in a grassy open area dotted with bushes and shrubs.

Suddenly I noticed a rhino trotting along parallel to the track some 50 metres away from the vehicles partially hidden by bushes. As we could see the people in the other car were not looking in his direction, we guessed they had not seen him. Without warning, the rhino turned 90 degrees and charged straight at Eck's vehicle. He hit it just behind the rear side door, about a foot from where our son David was sitting. The vehicle tipped right over on to two wheels on the opposite side and then landed back on all four wheels again. The rhino charged a second time – I think he hit the vehicle three times altogether, cutting open the metal side above the left rear wheel and smashing the rear side window. Eck attempted to get the car started and moving, but it seemed each time he tried to get going the wheels were off the ground from another rhino bash!

At last – it seemed an age though was probably less than a couple of minutes – he got going and set off at high speed, chased by the irate rhino. We sat open-mouthed watching all this, and Jobst wondered what to do. He considered charging the rhino to drive it away, but he worried that we might end up with two damaged vehicles and a very angry beast! After a short distance Eck, with great presence of mind, swerved sharply to the left around a bush, and the rhino kept on running straight!

We continued driving for about half a kilometre to make sure we were well away from the rhino before stopping, to catch our breath and assess the damage! The rhino had cut himself quite badly in his fierce attack as blood was spattered over the side and rear of the Land Rover. The force he had used, which almost tipped the vehicle right over, had resulted in the two right hand side tires being almost forced off their rims. They were stuffed full of earth and grass where they had gouged into the sides of the track.

We all dined off that story for quite a while, and Eck proudly continued to drive around in his Land Rover, with its side split open as though by a tin opener, for several weeks before getting it repaired! As for our keen photographer friend – it had all happened so suddenly and unexpectedly – he completely forgot to take a photo. Our son David did get a bit of a wobbly shot with his Box Brownie before he dived over to the far side of the vehicle to get as far away as possible from the charging rhino.

Sadly, shortly after this happened poachers slaughtered all the rhinos in Ruaha National park and none remain today.

Liz de Leyser, Mbeya, Tanzania

A Fishy Story

Eric Bowyer, proprietor of the Naivasha Stores, found a strange-looking fish caught by accident in J D Hopcraft's tilapia net in March 1930. The fish was gutted and dried and sent to Andrew McCrae in Nairobi. Before sending the fish, Bowyer wired McCrae asking him to have the fish identified by Van Someron at the museum. McCrae was living with Emil Jardin at the time. The fish arrived before the wire and Jardin assumed some friend had sent him a gift and he ate the fish. When McCrae later received the wire asking him to have the fish identified, Jardin had to dig through his dustbin to find the fish skeleton. They took it to Van Someron who identified it from the bones as a black bass. It was one of 56 that had been released into Lake Naivasha by Dick Dent, Naivasha's Fish Warden, a year earlier in February 1929.

Mervyn Carnelly from his informal history of Naivasha

Python Tug-of-War

As Captain William Barton and his daughter Margaret read books by the sand at Likoni, he heard a loud squeal from his dachshund puppy, Betty. Captain Barton rushed to the nearby coral rocks and saw Betty's rear legs disappearing down a hole. "I dived after her," Captain Barton said, "and with my head and shoulders down the hole, managed to get hold of her legs. At that time I couldn't see what had her. My daughter Margaret then came along and tried to help me, but we could not get the dog out. My daughter then ran up to house to get my son." Shortly after this Captain Barton managed to see what was gripping the dog. "Looking down the hole I could see a large python with the dog's head caught firmly in its jaws. Behind it I could see coil after coil of snake."

Captain Barton began to tire from the struggle, but a more dangerous threat arrived. A swarm of bees, roused by the battle, swarmed around Captain Barton's head, stinging him. Captain Barton said, "I couldn't hold on any more, but I decided to have one last try. I suddenly let go of the dog's legs and managed to get my fingers around her chest with my fingers interlocked. I could feel the saliva from the snake squirting over my hands as it tried to swallow the dog. I was almost at the breaking point when I gave one last mighty pull. The dog came free – but she didn't come to me first. She dashed at the snake and tore it open twice under its jaws and then she jumped into my arms. Betty then dashed off into the water to prevent the bees from stinging her."

Captain Barton, his legs and arms badly lacerated from being dragged on the coral rocks, had just moved away from the hole when his son, Dr Bill Barton who was visiting on leave, arrived with help. He, too, had to run into the ocean to avoid the bees. Captain Barton's wounds were dressed and Betty also received first aid for the cuts from the snake's bite.

Captain Barton, who had retired to Likoni after a career as a captain on steamships in Uganda's lakes, said of the event: "It was the worst ten minutes of my life."

Submitted by Dr Bill Barton, Nairobi

Lion on the Racetrack

At an early race meeting in Nairobi in 1903 a lion chased a zebra across the track as the race was in progress. The jockeys are said to have ridden the fastest races of their careers, although a number of them never made the finishing post as their mounts turned on seeing the lion in possession of the freshly killed zebra.

*Excerpted from **White Hunters** by Brian Herne*

Where the Elephant Sank

A permanent settlement at Dodoma came into existence in 1910 when the Germans and the central railway line arrived. At the time the area was known as Idodomya, which in the Kigogo language means "the place where it sank," referring to an incident when an elephant drinking in a nearby pond got stuck in the mud. Idodomya went on the map as Dodoma.

*Taken from **Journey Through Tanzania** by Mohamed Amin, Duncan Willetts and Peter Marshall*

Crocodile Tales

I went on safari with my dad to Archer's Post to inspect one of his camel abattoirs. Even though the large slaughterhouse was pretty clean, I felt it was gross with death everywhere. They brought the camels in from the large corral and the 'executioner' would hold this stun gun – a kind of pistol that fired blanks that drove a small metal rod a half-inch into the front of the skull – against the camel's head. There would be a report and the camel would fall. The men quickly skinned the camel and cut it into sections. There were rows of metal tables around the floor that sloped slightly down to a drain where all the blood and stomach contents flowed down into a near-vertical tube and into the Ewaso Ngiro river – where a large number of crocodiles had gathered for the feast.

As I walked around looking at everything, I slipped on the slimy sloping edge of the drain! Wsheeeeeew – I scooted along the downhill drain sending up a spray of blood and guts and small bits and pieces of camel, heading for the outlet pipe at a terrific rate. I could see the crocodiles with open jaws waiting to gulp me down as a nice titbit!

As I skidded towards the drain tube, a strong black arm shot out from nowhere at the last instant and grabbed me by the elbow and stopped me! A worker hauled me out, dripping with gore but so very happy to still be alive! The workers gathered round to inspect me. They washed me and I put on some spare clothes from my dad's car. After that, they fitted a big grill over the outlet pipe so no one would fall into the crocodiles' dinner plate!

Oscar Mann, Nairobi

Raiders in the Ostrich Pen

Last year, two breeders completed an ostrich enclosure, which they felt was so secure that they might rest happy in their beds.

The *boma* was perhaps 40 yards square, and consisted of huge posts some 10 feet high and was bound together by strands of barbed wire within and without at intervals of three or four inches. In all there were more than seven miles of barbed wire around it. Outside, again, was a fence of thorns, in itself almost impenetrable. Nevertheless, the settlers' confidence was misplaced. One morning they were roused with the unwelcome tidings that five lions had visited the enclosure, had slain fifty odd out of seventy ostriches contained therein, and had then decamped — all save one, who was too swollen to retreat through the gap by which he entered. The captive dispatched, an inspection was made, and the fury with which the lions had made their attack on the boma was evidenced by the blood and fur strewn about. The gap had been formed by literally tearing with teeth and claws the wire from its supports and eventually forcing open a narrow hole. Nor was this all. Next morning the boy who brought the early tea remarked, "Tea, sir, and another big lion in the *boma*!" Running out in pyjamas, another fine male was found unable to locate the means of egress and was shot, which experience was repeated on two subsequent days! The skins of the dead beasts were found torn and scratched in every direction by the barbs.

Lord Cranworth in his 1912 book, **A Colony in the Making**

A Crocodile Tail

My hunting partner Jim shot a crocodile on a tributary of the Tana River. The dead croc drifted downstream and grounded on a sand bank. We hauled it up on the bank for skinning. We saw where Jim's bullet had entered just above the crocodile's eye.

Our men tried unsuccessfully to cut through the crocodile's horny armour plating. Jim decided to show them how it was done. He turned the crocodile upside down, took the tail between his legs and jabbed the blade of his knife into the soft under skin. The tail gave a convulsive flick sending Jim flying headlong into the river. The crocodile was dead, but Jim had touched off a muscular reflex with surprising results!

From H K Binks' book, **African Rainbow**

Bugs in a Tin

An Englishman serving in the Colonial Police in Kenya's remote Northern Frontier District became obsessed with the insects that committed suicide by flying into his soup. He took a large Jacobs Biscuit tin on safari with him. He never sat down to a meal without the tin on the table. As insects dive-bombed his soup and drowned, he fished them out and carefully put them in the tin. It was his only entertainment. Rare visitors had to endure long accounts of how, during the rainy season of a certain year, he had filled the tin in a fortnight, whereas the present season was not so favourable. Although shatteringly boring to the visitor, the policeman found the topic positively exciting.

From Jennifer Stutchbury's unpublished manuscript, **Time's Eye**.

Leopard Crashes Engagement Party

Peter Lavers came to Kenya in 1926 and took a job on a coffee farm in Limuru. At a musical evening he met Jean Miller, on staff at Limuru Girls' School. They fell in love so Peter decided to ask Jean to marry him. On a wet night he took Jean for a ride in his Model T Ford. The car's radiator boiled over furiously. Peter stopped and hiked down to a nearby stream and collected water in his pith helmet to pour into the radiator. Peter decided this was the perfect moment to propose marriage. They talked about marriage for a few minutes and Jean agreed to be his wife. Peter walked back to the stream to get one last helmet full of water to top up the radiator. He screwed on the cap. As he climbed into the car a terrific crash on the roof rocked the Model T. A full-grown leopard had leapt on the roof, splitting it right across. The leopard hopped onto the bonnet and bounded into the night.

After they both caught their breath, Jean looked at Peter and said, "Well, that was nearly a very short engagement!"

*Adapted from **Memories of Kenya**, submitted by David Morseby Cunningham, Malindi*

Buffalo Attacks Bicycle

Living on Kianzabe Coffee Estate on the foothills of Donyo Sabuk Mountain was an exciting life. Buffaloes came off the mountain from time to time and thundered through the coffee smashing the trees and doing untold damage. My husband Peter Davey, manager on the farm, often had to drive the buffaloes back up the mountain, usually by shooting over their heads.

One morning at 6:30 am, a tractor driver from the estate missed roll call. Peter Davey noted the driver's absence as he assigned the workers their different tasks for the day. As everyone headed for their jobs, a very agitated, very scared and very grey looking tractor driver ran into the factory compound, yelling "*Mbogo! Mbogo!*"

Peter managed to quieten the driver down so he could tell his story. The driver had been cycling through the coffee to work, as he lived off the farm, when he suddenly heard a thudding noise behind him. He looked round to see a big bull buffalo coming down the same row of coffee! He panicked and fell off his bike and jumped to the side. The buffalo charged at the bike and was now rushing through the coffee with the bike attached to his horns, causing mayhem.

On hearing the story Peter rushed home to get his gun. Now he had the frightening task of looking for this very irate buffalo. Luckily, the buffalo was easy to spot galloping through the coffee with his head held high and the bike festooned on his horns. Once the buffalo was dead, they retrieved a very mangled bike from the buffalo's horns. The workers were happy to get a month's supply of meat in one day.

Grete Davey, Nairobi

Lutembe the Crocodile

"Lutembe! Lutembe!" called the old Ugandan fisherman, waving a fish by the shore of Lake Victoria. We had come to this spot between Entebbe and Kampala in 1927 having heard about this fisherman's special relationship to an old crocodile.

As we watched, a faint ripple on the lake surface gradually widened and soon the loathsome-looking crocodile heaved itself onto the beach and lay facing us expectantly. The fisherman threw his fish one at a time into Lutembe's snapping jaws. At the end of his feast, the croc returned to the water. The old fisherman ran up and lifted the end of Lutembe's tail like a trainbearer. I saw Lutembe perform several times over the next few years on family outings. Lutembe's photographs appeared in the **Illustrated London News**, bringing the crocodile worldwide fame. Gradually Lutembe's appearances became less predictable and eventually he disappeared.

From Alice Boase's book, ***When the Sun Never Set***

Feeding Lutembe the Crocodile

In about 1949 when I was visiting some people in Entebbe, they asked if I'd like to feed the crocodile in Lake Victoria. I was a bit shattered at the suggestion, knowing crocodiles are particularly partial to human flesh! However, they explained this particular crocodile, named Lutembe, expected only fish (either dead or alive) and we all set off to the lakeshore.

First one had to buy a supply of fish and I wondered if this was a scam for the local people to sell more fish. We bought the fish and a horde of people accompanied us as we headed for a certain place on the lakeshore calling out, "Lutembe, Lutembe!"

Before long Lutembe appeared, almost at my feet, with its mouth wide open. I was almost too terrified to remember the fish I'd brought, but shouts from the onlookers reminded me. I quickly threw fish to him. When Lutembe had consumed all the fish, it closed its mouth and disappeared back into the deep.

Jane Barnley, Kitale, Kenya

Rhino Encounter

Back in the early 1960s when I was newly married, my husband Joe and I spent many happy weekends with the Aagaard family at Yatta Ranch off the Garissa road. Their son Finn was Joe's best friend and on Sundays we would go hunting down in the Seven Forks area of the Tana River. We were usually looking for an impala or other meat for the pot. One man would carry a light rifle for the small game and the other would carry a .375 in case we had a problem with buffalo. Both men held game licences as laws were very strict. In those days there were very few people in the area. It was hot and dry and the bush was full of wait-a-bit thorns.

On one occasion as we walked through a clearing, a rhino suddenly appeared from out of the wait-a-bit. Finn quickly jumped behind a small tree on the left and Joe hid behind another on the right. I stood in the middle of the clearing and decided that as rhino are so shortsighted, maybe it was best to stand perfectly still! When Joe saw that I was about to be run over, he aimed the .375 and dispatched the rhino with a shot through the neck and shoulder. Much to his amazement, I didn't fling my arms around his neck in thankfulness. Instead, I asked with great concern, "What will the Game Department say?"

We eventually managed to turn the rhino over and found an arrowhead and shank, where the poison is wrapped, deeply embedded in its side. Two Wakamba men who had heard the shot came along hoping for some free meat. We left them with at least 1000 pounds of meat to shuttle back to their families. We carefully removed the arrowhead and the poison along with the rhino horn and reported the incident to the local Game Warden.

At least we had saved the poor rhino from a slow, painful death from poison.

Simonne Cheffings, Nairobi

Dinner Guests

The slaughter of pleuropneumonia-positive cattle at Karenga (in Uganda) also attracted lions from many miles around. One night the lions joined me for supper. In the evening we would usually light a campfire around which we would sit over a beer or a glass of whisky. If I was alone my driver and safari cook would join me. On this night hardly had the fire been lit than the rain came down, so I was forced to withdraw to my tent. After a long interval Waswa, my usually cheerful cook, brought the first course of my dinner to the tent from the uniport where he had been cooking. He put the plate down on the table but then, instead of returning to the uniport to prepare the next course, he sat on my camp bed without saying a word, looking strangely nervous. When I finished the soup I suggested he get the next course, but all he could do was point wordlessly outside.

I took his point and looked outside the tent. There by the light of the fire were six lions, lying contentedly in its warmth. A very long time passed before I got the next course.

From Roland Minor's memoir, **A Lot of Loose Ends – A Vet in Africa.**

Buffalo in Marsabit

Near the summit of Mount Marsabit a natural spring provided the whole boma with a piped water supply. One day this supply dwindled to a trickle and I went to investigate together with Frank Church, a police officer, and two askaris. A track snaked through the forest the mile or so to the spring and we had covered most of that distance when suddenly a buffalo head appeared over the next rise. Buffalo have been known to walk away from a confrontation with hunters and much later make a successful and totally unexpected charge from behind. They are also past masters of the art of concealment, and will suddenly appear as if from behind a blade of grass. Finally, to add to the danger of this animal, a .303 bullet cannot penetrate the front of solid bone, which the buffalo presents when head on. We stood with some trepidation, guns lowered but ready, in line abreast across the path. We hoped one of our rifles might find its mark in the neck behind the forehead if the buffalo decided to charge with its head lowered, but our best rifle was Frank's 10 mm Mannlicher, only slightly better than the .303 service rifles in the hands of the askari. I, of course carried my trusty .22. I can see that buffalo now, as clearly as if it were yesterday, and it seemed a very long time while we stared at each other, neither of us moving. Then he suddenly crashed off into the forest and we proceeded on our way. As we breasted the rise we saw he had been guarding four cows. Fortunately they had had no calves with them...

David Nicoll-Griffith, York, UK

Trampling on a Snake

During the Second World War I sent a telegram to my fiancé Jessie Dare, who served with her missionary parents in Tabora, Tanganyika, saying I would be in Dodoma for a few days en route to my army unit in Nairobi, and wanted her to come see me. With typical determination, she managed to get a ride on a goods train, sitting on a deck chair in the guard's van.

By phone, she had arranged to stay at the CMS mission station just outside Dodoma, where I could go to see her during the day. This I did – faithfully promising her archdeacon host that I would observe a 10 pm curfew and walk the few miles back to the military transit camp in town to sleep each night.

The first night was cloudy and dark but the road was easy to follow, being flanked by what I called 'milk bushes.' Walking in a sandy track made by car wheels, I suddenly trod on something soft. Switching on my flashlight, I saw that I was standing on a puff adder! The snake, although alive, did not swing up to attack me. The wheels of a passing car had broken its back, saving me from probable death.

Next morning, when Jessie's hosts heard what had happened, they arranged for me to spend the remaining nights in one of the mission guest rooms.

Ken Durman, USA

Treed by Lions

My Dad, affectionately called Pole Pole, was returning to Nyeri via Thomson's Falls when the rains started in earnest. The road became a running stream of water. Dad remembered a friend saying if it got really wet on the plains road past Curry's Farm, he should take the top road through Deighton Downs, spend the night, then continue the next day to Nyeri.

With the rain pouring down, Dad decided to follow this advice. He turned right and headed into the forest towards the Aberdares. He came to a bridge over a small stream and crossed it in his old Model T Ford. The bridge collapsed behind him. He continued on through the heavy rain on the forest track and reached another stream in flood. When his Ford crept onto the bridge, it collapsed under him. He could drive no further. Dad climbed out and walked down the track as darkness fell. Fortunately, it had stopped raining.

He came to the Pacey River and forded it on foot, but missed the track on the other side and turned left instead of straight ahead. This left him walking onto the plains. By now it was dark. He thought he saw his friend's cook carrying a Dietz lantern and Dad shouted out. Instead of a lantern, Dad was surprised to see two luminous pairs of eyes looking at him. The eyes belonged to a lion and lioness which surrounded him and tried to herd him into the open plains.

Dad tried to make his way back to the forest. The lions followed and one kept trying to cut him off and turn him back to the plains. He reached the forest before the lions attacked and climbed a tree. Cramped and stiff, he spent the night in the tree while the lions sat at the base and looked up at him.

Dad must have dozed off and his walking stick, which he always used because of his old war wound, dropped to the ground and frightened the lions away. Shortly after that he noticed the eastern sky was lightening. Cold and stiff, he barely managed to climb out of the tree without falling. With great difficulty he began walking towards where the thought his friend's farmhouse would be.

As he came a round a corner with thick bush all around him, he stood face to face with a leopard! Waving his walking stick, he shouted at the leopard, which fortunately bounded into the bush. Dad continued on his way. Minutes later he saw the farmhouse ahead. He arrived in time for a 5 am breakfast. When he told his story, his farmer friend say they normally had no lions on the farm, but on the day before his herd boy had reported seeing two lions on the plains.

Peter Evans, ex-Nyeri

Baboon Sentinels at Airfield

Harry Brittain's book ***By Air*** (1933) had a picture of a baboon and a monkey, which were kept at the Dodoma airport. Their job was to give an advance warning if lions or leopards were trespassing in the area.

East African Standard, March 8, 1958

Lions Visit the Show

Shortly after Independence I, with the help of my friends,

organised a Son et Lumiere show called 'The African Night' on the tourist circuit of the Ngong Hills about twenty miles out of Nairobi. The audience would arrive by car or minibus from Nairobi and we optimistically had seating for one hundred visitors. The backdrop to the sound and light show was a rock face of the Rift Valley and the twenty amateur actors in appropriate costumes were appropriately illuminated as the pre-recorded voice told the history of Kenya. Nothing was more annoying than when the lights were dimmed and the voice penetrated the stillness of the African night with "Roll back the centuries, let time unfurl..." and then for the scene to be lit up with the headlights of the car of some late arrivals and usually with a blowing exhaust! We therefore had a notice posted two hundred yards from the site – 'Please leave your car here. Our staff will escort you.'

At 22:00 hours that moonless night the show was over, the applause died down and around fifty delighted clients collected the blankets they had been advised to bring and headed back to their cars. At 22:05 hours we heard the first scream. Six grown lions were sauntering in the pitch black around the 25 parked cars and one or two of them were walking up and down the track. I grabbed one of our megaphones and assured everyone in the pitch darkness that lions only eat people as a last resort when no other food is available. My encouraging words did not go down very well. However, we had a happy ending and the lions harmed no one.

Dick Hedges, Nairobi

African Vermin

General Sir George Erskine, General Officer Commander in Chief in Kenya in the Mau Mau Emergency, visited George Murray in 1955 at Marania farm near Timau. General Erskine enquired on how the sheep were. Murray replied that his sheep were much troubled by vermin. The General, thinking vermin to be mice or rats, asked: "What vermin?" Murray replied: "Lions!"

JPT Foster, taken from his historical paper on the settlement of Timau

Locating a Lion

My mother Shelina Popat worked in the Maasai Mara in tourism as a 22-year-old. One day a VIP guest, a middle-aged woman, arrived from England. She was very eager to see a lion. After her first game drive, the woman went to Shelina and explained that she really wanted to see a lion and she was only staying for three nights. Shelina told the woman not to worry, since lions were frequently seen.

But for some reason the Mara's lions went on strike that week and by the woman's last night, she still had not seen a lion. The woman kept complaining how she came all the way from England to see a lion and how disappointed she was. The woman had only one more game drive the next morning. When she came back from her last game drive, she still hadn't seen a lion. Feeling very dissatisfied, she went back to her tent to prepare to leave for the airstrip.

Shelina drove the woman to the airstrip to drop her off. However, on the way to the airstrip the woman needed to relieve herself. Shelina drove her to a location known for being deserted with no wild animals roaming about. She stopped the car in front of a large bush. The woman got out to go pee, while Shelina waited in the car. A loud scream erupted from behind the bush. The woman appeared, running towards the car with her shorts around her ankles, screaming, "Lion!"

Shelina couldn't help but laugh. The woman was terrified but also delighted. She finally saw a lion, even though not in the most appropriate circumstances.

Talisa Lanoe, International School of Kenya

Elephant Tales

When I worked in Tanzania constructing the TANZAM railway, elephants used to come into our camp in Mikumi to listen to classical music on the record player and drink water from our drums. One old bull attached himself to the earth-moving unit and used to get in the way because he had very poor eyesight. One day the old bull was grazing near an earth scraper on which I was working. He came across my red Thermos flask, which I had placed in the shade of a small bush. He sniffed the flask and then very carefully pulled the shady bush out of the ground, tapped it on his legs to remove the soil and swallowed it. He stepped carefully around the flask and went on his way!

Another day the driver of a Bedford lorry parked it and fell asleep in the cab as he waited for some men working on a culvert. A couple of the men finished their task and crawled beneath the truck for a snooze in the shade. The old bull elephant stuck his trunk through the window and sniffed the driver. He woke up with a fright, started the truck and reversed, running over the legs of one of the men underneath.

Another time a very excitable Italian foreman was beckoning to a tractor driver as he himself walked backwards. The driver began pointing vigorously back at the foreman. At the last moment the foreman turned around to see the old bull elephant standing right behind him. The foreman needed a change of shorts!

Peter Humphreys, Auckland, New Zealand

Snake in the Post Box

When we arrived to work near Marigat, we enquired about a post box. "Oh, a post box? You must make your own and put it on the veranda of the DO's office." Sure enough, we went to look and saw a row of a dozen little boxes of all shapes and sizes standing, vulnerable and colourful, on the open veranda. I made a box, painted it red, bought a tiny padlock and our postal arrangements were completed.

One memorable day I picked up our box, placed it on the low wall and opened it. Trustingly, I picked up the top layer of letters and there, wiggling its little black forked tongue at me, was a snake! I yelled to a nearby *askari* for help. He picked up my red box and heaved it out onto the muddy road. The snake slithered away and I scuttled out to prevent those few not-yet-muddy letters from being blown into the puddles. The rough handling had broken my box to smithereens, so I got someone more skilled than I to make another.

Lorna Eglin, Hermanus, South Africa

Buffaloes in the Maize

In the early 1950s elephants and buffalo raiding the Kikuyu shambas along the Aberdare forest edge had become a major problem, and so the Administration organised the hand-digging of a game ditch to try and stop this. Meanwhile, the Administration gave some of the affected people some thunder flashes to scare the raiding animals back into the forest. They were shown how to light the firework and advised to quickly throw it; and thereby hangs a tale.

One day a farmer heard some buffalo had entered his maize shamba, so he collected his recently-issued thunder flash and went to deal with the situation. He carefully approached the herd, lit the fuse and hurled the firework at the buffalo. But he had gotten too close to them in the maize, and threw the thunder flash so hard it landed beyond the animals. Realising his error, he turned to flee. Immediately after the loud bang, the buffalo herd thundered towards him. What to do? A large kei-apple hedge surrounded the *shamba*. Ignoring all the thorns, the farmer dove underneath it, just before the buffalo hurtled over the top.

Richard Truran, Devon

Raising a Racket

A farmer in Trans Nzoia had been playing tennis with his next-door neighbour. Their houses were only a short distance apart and he walked back to his house at dusk along a path through the long grass. He saw what he thought was a snake across the path. He hit it hard with his tennis racket. A furious roar erupted from a lion whose tail he had just thumped. Both lion and farmer made a hasty exit.

John Davies, Watamu

Lion in the Darkness

When I was in high school in the 1950s I went to help my Uncle Tom during school vacation. He was putting up radio transmitters at Lolkasali near Arusha and at Kibaya near Mt Meru. On that trip we crossed Maasai land where the Naberera Wells are a watering point deep below the ground. Two paths spiral down to the well. Cattle go down one and come up the other. As a kid I'd seen a picture of the wells in a schoolbook. On this trip we ran out of water and went to the wells to fill the radiator. On the Kibaya trip fixing transmitters we had a little grass hut about ten feet square. Pat, another young man on the crew, and I stayed on our own in the hut. We heard grunting at night and looked out to see a lion walking around the flimsy hut. Pat hissed at me, "Climb onto the roof truss." He grabbed a stick of dynamite with a fuse and detonator. "All I can do is drop this if the lion comes in," he said. Fortunately the lion didn't enter.

Lu Wedd, Naivasha

Camp Intruder

During the First World War an Indian Sapper regiment started on the railway to Maktau. When it got about halfway, the 25th Fusiliers arrived from Britain and they started making trenches and gun emplacements. They cut trees round about and, as I was at this time driving a three-ton Commer lorry, I used to chase through the bush and collect the timber they had cut. There was quite a lot of sniping on this road and when the Baluchis first went there, several sentries were shot at night with the result that they became very nervous.

The Baluchis piled a lot of bush against the gate so they should not be seen from the outside, but one night a guard heard something outside and looked up to see something looking down at him. He simply cried out and collapsed. I happened to drive the first car in that morning and had to take him, with the help of two other Baluchis, to Voi Hospital. He was quite out of his mind. If he ever got better, I don't know. What had put the wind up him was a giraffe that had walked up to the gate and looked over it.

From an unpublished memoir compiled by Anne (Johansen) Robertson. This section is about early Kenya settler Olaf Johansen. When Olaf was 22 in 1915 he joined the East Africa Transport Crew in WWI.

He carried supplies to Maktau where Baluchis and the King's African Rifles were stationed. Submitted to Old Africa by Esther Shaffer.

Mombasa's Giant Tortoise

The Manor Hotel in Mombasa was the home of Liza, a giant land tortoise said to be 250 or 300 years old. Legend had it the Portuguese brought the tortoise to Mombasa. Liza could be seen plodding infinitely slowly to Mbaraki Creek along the road to Likoni ferry, and occasionally she forsook the Manor for the Castle Hotel. One day, oblivious to traffic, Liza was napping in the shade behind a taxi in the rank beside the Castle Hotel. The taxi driver failed to see Liza and reversed over her, cracking her shell. Liza staggered back to the Manor, where she hung on to life for a month and then died. All Mombasa mourned when she met her end. Liza's shell, lovingly and regularly polished by the staff, was displayed in the Manor foyer.

Christine Nicholls, Oxford

A Green Girl and her .22 Rifle

I was four or five months pregnant with our first child, Hugh was away for the day, and I was alone at the farm, when one of the men came running to me, breathless and excited.

"*Kuja Memsab. Kuleta bunduki. Kwa kuua nyama*," he said. "Come Memsab, bring the gun to kill meat." I did not ask them what the meat was. I thought they wanted me to shoot a buck.

"*Wapi?*" I asked, "Where?"

"*Kuja, kuja*," and they started to run. I got my .22 rifle and followed, more slowly, where they led, quite a long way into the forest.

"*Pole pole, pole pole, ako hapa*," they cautioned. "Slowly, slowly, it's here."

We found a buffalo lying in a clump of bushes. It was very large and snorting with anger. It had been hamstrung by the Africans and was unable to move, I hoped. I had never been so close to a buffalo before. I was pretty green, but I knew a .22 would never penetrate a buffalo hide. There was only one way, so with a steady hand I shot it straight through the eye. He died instantly.

"I shot a buffalo this afternoon," I told Hugh when he returned to the house.

"Good Heavens! What with?"

"My .22," and I told him the story…I was ragged for years as the green girl from England who went out to shoot a buffalo with a .22 rifle.

Lorna Hindmarsh, taken from her memoir **Beyond Happy Valley**

Riled Up Rhinos

On the eve of World War 2 I joined the King's African Rifles (KAR). At Isiolo a thorn-bush covered hillside to the west had been set aside as a field firing range where the troops used live ammunition. One unit set out the targets – white six-inch square steel plates – and another unit later went into the area shooting at every plate they saw. At the end the plates were collected and a count made: how many bullets fired and how many hits registered.

On one occasion my unit, "D" Company of the 1st KAR, set out the steel plates. "A" Company of the 5th battalion went in to shoot them up. The troops formed a long line abreast across the slope on the bare hillside and advanced, rifles ready. Firing soon started and gradually increased in intensity. The shooting suddenly stopped and the line of troops galloped out of the bush with six very irate rhinos charging after them! On reaching open ground, the annoyed rhinos paused, snorted and pawed the ground before trotting off. That ended field firing for the day.

Karl Johansen, taken from a family history called **Ujamaa Wetu** *written by Anne Freeman Robertson (nee Johansen) and edited by Jeanette Anne Robertson, New Brunswick, Canada*

Leaping Pythons

When I was fourteen years old I visited my friends the Renners in Tanganyika who lived on a remote mission station near Singida. It was primarily a leprosarium where the patients had their own houses and planted their own gardens. For one of my jobs I rode a horse up through the village to see if the patients had any special needs. A small dam near the station held a lake of brown water. In the mornings I would sometimes take an old dugout canoe and paddle across the lake and up the narrow feeder stream. One day as I paddled near a high bank

I heard a rustling in the grass above me and suddenly a dozen small pythons leapt over my head and into the water. It was an unnerving experience and I left the area as quickly as possible.

However, I was curious, so the next day I paddled the canoe to the same area to see if the pythons had returned. I watched the banks carefully and as I negotiated a bend in the river I spotted a gigantic python resting on the bank below a gnarled tree. I figured it must be the mother of the small pythons that had flown over my head. I didn't want to face this large python alone. I reversed direction and when I got to the shore I ran all the way to the hospital where Dr Moris was seeing patients. He had the only gun on the station and I begged him to come and kill the giant python. He finally agreed. He left his patients and went to his house where he picked up his 12-gauge shotgun and we ran down to the river. We approached the location of the python on land – walking as quietly as we could. Rounding a thicket I could see the gigantic python had not moved. We were about 50 paces away and I pleaded with Dr Moris to shoot. He raised the shotgun and aimed – but then he hesitated and lowered the gun. He said we needed to get closer. We crept to within 30 paces. Again, Dr Moris lifted the shotgun and then put it down. He said we needed to get even closer. This time we crept to within 10 paces. When we stood up it was suddenly obvious we were not looking at a gigantic python. We were looking at a large twisted root. I was terribly embarrassed. I had pulled the good doctor away from his work. All for a twisted root.

Jon Arensen, Houghton, New York

Buffalo Pulls Off Car Door

Years ago when the Nairobi National Park was young, and the animal orphanage recently installed and operating, they released some buffalo into the Nairobi National Park. These buffalo were rather tame having been around humans for a time. Soon after the release of the buffalo, an Asian man visiting the park drove into the forest area of the park and came upon this group of tame buffalo and stopped his small vehicle. One of the buffalo made his way over to the car. The visitor was excited to see a buff but it came too close! This buffalo came right up to the vehicle and shoved one horn through the window of the driver's side. This forced the driver to shift quickly into the front passenger seat. The buff manoeuvred his other horn in. With the buffalo's head and both horns in the small car, the driver didn't know what to do! After a few moments the buff wanted to pull his head out, but couldn't. He was locked in by his horns. In a panic the buff dug his forelegs into the earth and gave a tremendous pull and yanked the door entirely off! The buff retreated to his grazing wearing the car door as a necklace around its neck! The driver hastened to the gate to report the incident and collect a game scout or two. When they arrived back at the scene, the buff had managed to dislodge the door from its neck and was happily grazing with the others. They recovered the car door, but I don't know whether it was in good enough shape to be put back on the car or if it had to be replaced with another.

John Davies, Watamu, as told to Van E Davis, Malindi

Jezebel and the Puff Adder

When living outside Naivasha on the edge of the Rift Valley in a somewhat lonely and rugged place, we didn't have too many wild animals, but we did have snakes. One morning Ezekiel, our *mpishi* and the chap who totally ran the household, rushed in to say Jezebel, one of our dogs, had been bitten by a *nyoka*. Hastily putting our baby daughter and Ayah plus the dogs into our old blue Vanguard, we drove off down the very bumpy track to Naivasha to take Jezebel to the Veterinary station. Driving perhaps too quickly through a flooded *donga*, the car stalled in the middle. With no one nearby to help, we got out and opened the bonnet. We removed the spark plugs one by one and dried them off with the only dry cloth we had – one of the baby's nappies. By a miracle, the car started. We arrived at the Vet to find no one there. By now Jezebel was unconscious, the fang marks clearly visible on her lip. We took Jezebel to the District Hospital where the Matron, after a little hesitation, injected our dog near the heart. In a very short time Jezebel recovered. We returned home and found our workers, with great jubilation, had killed the six-foot-long puff adder that had bitten Jezebel.

Daphne Johnson, Hereford, UK

South of the Tana

In the 1960s I helped run logistics for a film crew from Denmark making a film called *South of the Tana*. We ran a camp for the movie crew on the Tana River. The plot involved a girl coming to Africa to find her father who had disappeared. She finds him poaching elephants, but he is being forced to do it by a real crook who heads up the poaching operations. The finale of the film was a scene where the girl's father fought with the head poacher and he fell into the Tana River to be eaten by a crocodile. We had to provide the crocodile. X Matthews shot a large croc and we floated it to the edge of the river and tied its feet together. Then by flipping the feet, we were able to make the crocodile glide through the river for the part of the film shooting where the crocodile stalks the villain. For the scene where the crocodile actually attacks, we opened the croc's mouth and put in a stick to keep it open, to make it look like it was ready to bite the villain. The first film shot wasn't good enough for the direction, so he asked us to do it again. This time, just as we manoeuvred the open-mouthed croc near the villain, the stick broke. The crocodile's teeth-studded mouth flopped shut on the movie actor's thigh. He thought the crocodile had come back to life and screamed and yelled and rushed out of the river. Nothing could persuade him to shoot the scene again. The film wasn't much of a success, but we heard later it was shown on television in Denmark.

Paul Herd

Rhino Cargo

In 1949 Col George Jazman was driving his 10 cwt Fordson panel van on the Kiganjo-Mweiga road from his house between Monte Carlo Ranch and Steep (now Aberdare Country Club) when he heard a huge thump in the back of the car. He looked around and saw a rhino in his car! Luckily he was on his way to do his duty as the hunter for Treetops and had his rifle with him and was able, with great difficulty, to shoot his unwanted passenger before the rhino completely destroyed his car. A photo of the rhino in the car was printed in *Field* magazine.

David Doig, Njombe, Tanzania

Pythons on the Malewa

There were a lot of pythons along the Malewa River and we saw them all the time. As a youngster it was always amusing when I was sent off to take people fishing who were new to the country and watch their reactions on their first encounter with a python! The poor Colonel of the Coldstream Guards managed to put his foot right in the middle of a very large coiled python. It took some time to calm him down and he eventually started fishing. After the first pool he clambered up the bank after me and grabbed hold of a good thick branch to haul himself out of the river only for it to move! He had grasped a python! There was quite a splash and that ended fishing for that day. Pythons never bothered us and as I seldom wore shoes it was not unusual to feel them underfoot.

John Dawson, UK

Uganda Adventures

I had a small grey monkey...which was very tame and used to sit on the crossbar of my bicycle and accompany me wherever I went. I always remember the first time I went to my brother Robert's camp at Kaliro in Uganda. The monkey suddenly leapt on my head, cursing furiously. I wondered what on earth had upset him and then saw a half-grown leopard tied up to a tree. Robert came out and said that George had brought it over as the meat question was difficult where he was and Robert would be able to get meat easily for it. We patted the leopard and rubbed its head but we could not quieten the monkey, so I took him round to the back of the *banda* where he got another unpleasant shock, for sitting chained to a branch of a tree was a very large grey eagle. The leopard was quite tame, except when he was being fed, but nothing would ever induce the monkey to go near it. With the eagle it was quite different and the monkey soon got over his first shock and then the tables were turned and the eagle saw far too much of the monkey. The little devil would spend hours near the bird and whenever he got the opportunity he would dash in and try to grab some feathers out of its tail. The eagle, though quick, was never quite quick enough, and the monkey always managed to dodge its claws, which was lucky for the monkey for I doubt if we would have been able to get it out of the eagle's clutches before it was seriously injured, if not ripped to bits...Robert... told me that this was a very rare species of eagle. He later gave the eagle to the Governor, Sir Frederick Jackson...I have no idea what kind of eagle this was, and I have never seen one since, not even illustrated in books.

That night Robert told me that his cook had gone sick and he had sent out word that he wanted another. Early one morning a boy turned up with a letter of recommendation saying what a very fine cook he was, So Robert took him on. George was staying there at the time and as they had not had breakfast, Robert gave the new cook some Quaker oats, buck liver, bacon and tea and told him to get on with it and bring it in when all was ready. He and George were talking outside and, after a while, Robert feeling hungry looked inside the *banda* and seeing only a teapot on the table called the cook and asked why he was so long with breakfast. The boy looked surprised and said that he had brought it long ago. Robert told him not to be a fool and to hurry and bring the rest of the food. Did the cook expect that they would only have tea for breakfast? But the boy insisted he had brought everything to the table An awful thought struck Robert and he silently went across to the table and lifted the lid of the teapot…There in the teapot was a revolting sight – porridge, liver, tea and bacon all mixed together…

While at Kagwarra, Robert's leopard came to a sticky end. He had tied it up to the gateway of the rest house compound and one evening when he was away…a troop of baboons came towards the compound. The leopard, seeing them, crouched behind the hedge and when a young baboon came within reach, sprang at it and caught it. The infuriated baboons, hearing the yells of their young, turned on the leopard and literally tore it to pieces.

Hugh Foster in the book **Uganda Adventures** *published by his son*
Francis Foster

Baby Encounters Python

In 1957, my husband Jobst was building a boarding school at the small settlement of Chimala on the Great North road between Iringa and Mbeya. At the time we lived in Tukuyu, the Headquarters of Rungwe District and about 70 miles from Chimala over a mountainous, rather hair-raising road, which dropped down from the heights of the Poroto Mountains at over 7000 feet to the Usangu plains at around 3000 feet. Jobst sometimes had to spend two or three days at a time at Chimala.

Friends of ours, the Cormack family, ran a small hotel in Chimala, mostly catering for passing Great North road traffic. I occasionally took our baby son, Peter, and went with Jobst to stay at the hotel in Chimala.

One morning as we ate breakfast at the hotel in Chimala, a young herd boy ran in to say there was a large python on the land behind the hotel where he had been herding some of the Cormack's livestock – mostly calves and sheep. He had bravely speared the python and come running for help. We abandoned our breakfast and set off to look for the python – Jobst, Roma Cormack (the daughter of the hotel owners), myself carrying Peter and the herd boy with a wheelbarrow to carry the dead python.

On reaching the place where the herd boy had speared the python, we found the spear lying on the ground, but no snake. It had obviously shaken itself loose. After scouting around in the fairly thick bush we found the python half way up a tree. Jobst got hold of a stick, beat the python to the ground and then beat its head quite severely. The python appeared to be dead, so they lifted it up and coiled it into the wheelbarrow and took it down to the hotel. We stretched it out on hotel's driveway to measure it and I placed Peter on the ground close beside it and we took a photograph. Just as we had finished taking the photo, the python suddenly came to life and took off into the nearby flowerbed, much to everyone's consternation! I hastily snatched up my precious baby while someone hurriedly fetched a panga and cut off the python's head. On his return, Keith Cormack, the son of the house, scathingly said we should never have considered the python to be dead until it had been decapitated!

Liz de Leyser, Iringa

Elephants and Lions

I remember some special safaris to Marsabit with my parents when I was eight or nine years old. We once saw a herd of 600 elephants crossing the Uaso Nyiro River at the point which is now Samburu Safari Lodge. We also saw a lot of elephant and buffalo on Marsabit Mountain, and one of the largest old male elephants was Ahmed. We visited Joy and George Adamson at their home near Isiolo, and I can clearly remember Elsa as a small cub.

One night in 1951 about 20 elephants invaded our garden at Isiolo. My father blew his police whistle to frighten off the elephants – they were eating the pepper trees – and about five minutes later the whole of the Dubas Tribal Police contingent – some 50 policemen – came to our house by lorry from their Police Lines to help frighten the elephants away.

On another occasion, a young friend of mine (Shaun Metcalf) and I were sleeping in a tent in the garden and a lion prowled around our tent. We found the footprints in the mud the next day!

Tony O'Hagan, son of former P C Desmond O'Hagan, Northern Province in a letter to Mervyn Maciel after reading Maciel's book
Bwana Karani

A Near Miss

I was hunting in Block 60 in 1971 with my older brother Dave and a friend Mike Smalling. Block 60 was above the Maasai Mara. Dave had already shot a huge buffalo. I'd shot one as well, but we were determined to find a buffalo with an even bigger set of horns. We went out on foot looking for a big bull buffalo. We came to a very tall hill with a huge herd of buffalo at the top. The three of us made our way up through the thick brush on the side of the hill to get close enough to the herd to isolate a big bull and shoot it. Without warning the herd stampeded down the hill. There were at least 150 to 200 buffalo. Their thundering hooves shook the ground and the hillside filled with crashing noise. We panicked and ran down the hill looking for trees big enough to climb. I still remember how everything seemed to move in slow motion, even though we were running like mad. We could feel the vibrations of the noise and bushes scratched us as we ran.

Dave and Mike were in front of me. Both carried their .458 Winchester rifles. I had a .375 Sako, a gun David had recently acquired. Because we'd been so close to the buffalo, we had all locked and loaded and had bullets in our chambers. The Sako was a good gun for smaller game, but I didn't realize some moron had installed it with a hair trigger, set to go off at the lightest touch. I'd been trained in gun safety, so as I ran I carried the gun pointing down and was careful not to have my finger on the trigger. But somehow as we sprinted crazily through the thick bush, a branch must have touched the trigger and my gun fired. In that adrenalin-rush moment when everything seems to move slowly, I saw the air blast of the bullet as it ripped through the air and riffled the leg of my brother's trousers. To my immense relief the bullet didn't hit him or Mike. We scrambled up some small trees. The buffalo split into two groups and ran around us.

As we caught our breath and realised we were safe, Mike looked around and asked, "Did I hear a gun go off back there?"

"Oh no," I answered, hastily. "I didn't hear anything."

Dave said, "I didn't hear anything either."

I kept that secret to myself. I didn't have the heart to tell my older brother I'd almost shot him in our rush to escape from the buffalo. The moral of the story is, "Never get a rifle with a hair trigger."

Richard E Schaefer, Camarillo, California

The Thunderflash

It was a long time ago when friends of ours worked on a sisal plantation in Kibwezi, just far enough down the Mombasa Road to make a good long weekend trip worthwhile. Mike and Sue had a spacious house and many a good party was held there!

Now the sisal decorticators were large and noisy. Sisal leaves went in one end and white 'string' came out the other, while the wash was a green sludge fuel of nitrogen and other goodies, which Mike found was good for growing vegetables. He laid out a large vegetable garden surrounded by a thick euphorbia hedge (animal proof) and everyone enjoyed fresh vegetables. That is until two old buffalo smelled this garden of Eden on an otherwise dry Kibwezi landscape. They put their heads down, horns and boss forward and walked through the hedge! A very cross Mike ordered two askaris to do night watch! "Call me at once!"

We happened to be there that weekend with Mike's sister Pam and her boyfriend. After an afternoon of Pims and crisps and fun and laughter we sat down to dinner. Now Mike had taken the opportunity of going down to the duka in Kibwezi and asking Mr Patel if he had a thunderflash or anything similar. "Yes, Bwana. The army being leaving some of them here for me." A dusty box arrived from the back of the duka and lo and behold what looked like thunder flashes lay there! Delighted, Mike armed himself with two and went home.

Halfway through this dinner an out of breath and puffing askari arrived and said, "*Bwana, mbogo nafika.*"

The men scrambled, grabbing the thunderflashes, jackets and matches and shouted, "You girls stay here!"

Well, Pam and I did not want to miss the fun but Sue, Mike's wife, would not leave her dinner. She claimed she was scared of sparklers! So Pam and I, leaving a small time later, crept down the road and found an old D8 grader standing just where we could climb up and have a grand stand view.

Below us the veg garden was pitch black. It was a very cloudy night, but suddenly the clouds blew apart and a full moon shone down on a line up of five men and two buffalo about 20 feet away, mouths full of tender young carrots. Mike lit the flash and gave it quickly to Robert. "You can throw further," he said. Rob hurled it and it landed just under the nose of one buffalo. It ignited and lit up the whole place beautifully. It was a flare, not a thunderflash! The buffalo saw this line of men, lowered their heads, scraped the ground with one hoof (as they always do) and charged. The men scattered, some to the left and some to the right up the slope and I suppose into the decorticator shed. The clouds closed and it was total darkness again.

Pam and I clung together on top of the D8. We could hear snorting buff and knew we must not move and also knew we were in deep trouble! About ten minutes later we saw car lights coming from the house and we were collected and soundly told off! I'm not sure if it was because we had disobeyed or because we had seen it all and no tall stories could be made up by those intrepid hunters, but it's all water under the bridge now!

Shirley Poole, Naivasha, Kenya

Two Snake Stories

I had an amusing experience when I was Senior Assistant and Tea Factory Manager on Chemomi Tea Estate in Nandi Hills in 1959. One of our Nandi Cattle herdsmen came to me early one morning and said he had found a large python asleep some distance away and asked if I would like it. I said, "OK, but if you have to kill it, don't damage its head."

A few hours later he turned up at our house with a large sack over his shoulder, which he tipped out on the front veranda to reveal the front half of a python. It was 11 feet long with a relatively undamaged head – he had only used the spike on the back of his panga to neatly 'brain' it.

I asked him where the rest of the python was and he said as it was too heavy to carry, so he had cut it in half. I told him to go back and get the rest and I would pay him. Later he turned up empty handed and said the tail end half had disappeared – he thought wild dogs must have taken it.

A few days later at the Nandi Bears Club, Max Gamble, the manager of Savanni Estate, was telling everyone that a local Nandi worker had brought him the tail end half (which measured 12 feet) of a huge python he had found dead in the jungle. I said I had the front end, which measured 11 feet, and I had skinned it. Max said he had skinned and salted his half and sent it to the tannery at Nakuru, where I also had sent my half to be tanned. I eventually had six beautiful handbags made from it. At 23 feet that was the largest python I knew of, though Dr Leakey told me he had a record of a 26-footer from Uganda.

I still have the preserved skin of an 18 foot 6 inch python I got in Uganda in August 1963 when I was working on the Uganda Company's Mityiana Group Tea Estates some distance from our house. I had only been married in Kampala a couple of weeks prior to this episode.

After I got on my motorbike the estate workers carefully wound the dead python round me and secured it with a bit of rope. I proudly rode the bike home looking a bit like the 'Michelin Man' and my newly-wed Australian wife was surprised - to put it mildly. Fortunately, she has got used to my reptilian activities and we are just coming up to celebrate our 60th wedding anniversary!

Angus F. Hutton, Australia

Travelling Around East Africa

Goggling on the Mombasa Road

We cycled to Mombasa in 1966 for a beach holiday, starting from Rose Avenue in Nairobi. We had four in our group: David and Neil MacDonald, Colin Mitchell and myself. We started off on that wonderful downhill, past Nairobi Club, over the railway bridge and to Athi River, where the tarmac stopped – we were not to enjoy that luxury again until MacKinnon Road. We cycled on the red powdery dust of the Ulu Hills. One always talks of going 'down' to the Coast, but of course there are many uphills. Sultan Hamud was our first night stop and we asked the police if we could camp in their grounds; they were most welcoming and suggested we sleep in an empty cell for our own safety; there were some cattle-related skirmishes going on. We had a safe albeit interrupted night; in the early hours we heard a lot of *maneno* and soon the remaining cells filled up.

We made an early start the next morning while it was still dark. We rode through an area with many animals equipped with nothing but water pistols filled with ammonia. We felt sure this would put-off any large-sized animal from coming close to us. Our rather sad bicycle lights beamed at most 15 feet ahead and we heard real or imaginary noises in the bush. The four of us wobbled along the sandy road, squirting jets of ammonia into the air, shouting into the darkness.

Daylight brought a new problem; every time a lorry or car passed, we were covered in clouds of red, eye-watering, choking dust. Fortunately, since we were ready for our coast holiday, we had goggles and snorkels and we donned this equipment. What an odd sight we must have been, cycling in the heat of the day wearing our goggles and snorkels. We looked even odder when removed the goggles later to see our *wazungu* faces surrounded by dark brown, caked, sweaty dust. We spent a night of luxury at Tsavo Inn, but to economise we piled into one bed.

Seeing elephants from a car is a different experience from being on a bicycle – in those days, there were a lot of elephant around Manyani. Viewing the original railway bridge at Tsavo River was a memorable event. I remember our joy when we reached tarmac again at Mackinnon Road. The stony, corrugated part near Mariakani was probably the worst and made for very rough cycling, but we had that 'coast' feeling on us. And what bliss to see the sea in the distance – the long, downhill tarmac, exhilarating, freewheeling from Mazeras to the Causeway. We gingerly rode across the Nyali Bridge with its planks and sharp nails, but we made it to Nyali without one puncture. We had a wonderful holiday, with one night out at the Mombasa Drive-In cinema, after cycling back up the hill after the Causeway). We opted for the lazy way back to Nairobi; we took the 3rd class, daylight train, bikes and all. And then we had the final uphill from Nairobi Railway station to home.

Michael Nicholson, Hampshire, UK

Zebra Fat for Motor Oil

In the late 1940s our family was driving across the Kedong Valley when our Model A Ford broke down. We sat next to our car as evening approached, certain we'd have to spend the night. A Model T Ford sputtered up to us, steam spewing from its radiator. "Do you have any water?" the driver asked. We did, but as it was getting late the driver and his friend decided to spend the night camped next to our broken down car. The next morning after breakfast we topped up their radiator. Then to our amazement, they set a charcoal fire underneath their engine. As the flames rose up around the bottom of their engine, we asked, "What in the world are you doing?" The driver smiled. Not only had they run out of water, they'd run out of oil as well. But they had shot a zebra on their trip, so they rendered the zebra fat into an orange-red oil and poured it into their engine. "The zebra fat congeals overnight, so we're melting it down," the driver explained. After a while he checked the dipstick. Pronouncing the zebra fat now warm enough to serve as engine oil, they cranked the Model T to life and drove away.

Dilly Andersen, Timau

Guest of Honour Stuck in Nakuru Mud

Sir Peter Scott, the internationally renowned ornithologist and artist, cut the ribbon to officially open the Lake Nakuru Bird Sanctuary in February 1961. Scott described Lake Nakuru as "a sight of incredible beauty and interest…there can be no more remarkable ornithological sight in the world."John and Helen Start attended the ceremony and captured the moment with their camera. As Scott posed with scissors ready he said to the press photographers, "Have you all got your photos? This looks much better before I cut the tape."

After the opening, the governor took Peter Scott for a drive in his heavy Rolls Royce round the lake. At one point the car broke through the soda crust and sank into the ooze. Everyone had to get out and push, getting his or her shoes covered in the soda mud, which turns white when it dries.

That evening Scott was due to give a talk in the Nakuru Town Hall, but owing to the mud, he was late and had no time to change. He walked onto the stage still wearing his whitened trousers and shoes. He started his talk by apologising for being late saying, "I'm only just back from the Arctic and I still have snow on my boots!"

John and Helen Start, Roleystone, Australia

Piano to the Rescue

When I lived at Mumias I had a small piano brought up from the coast. The transport involved a great deal of labour. The piano was carried part of the way by porters and part of the way it was hauled in a bullock cart. In 1900 I was ordered by Colonel Ternan to build a new headquarters for the province in Kisumu where the railway would have its terminus. I packed the piano in its case and it lay in storage unused. Mr P H Clarke later offered to buy it from me so he could resell it in Uganda.

I agreed and he left one day from Kisumu for Entebbe in a sailing dhow with the piano as cargo. About a week later he staggered into my office, exhausted. He told me they had encountered a bad storm on the lake after leaving Kisumu. It was night and the dhow sank and the travelers were dumped into the water. Clarke swam around for a while before bumping against the piano, which was floating. Soon the African boat captain also clung to the piano case. The rest of the crew were never seen again. Clarke and the captain hung onto the piano and floated until daylight. They discovered they were a few miles from an island. They swam and pushed their unusual life preserver and finally landed on the beach in their piano boat. Some African fishermen picked them up and carried them back to the mainland.

A friendly chief, Ugada Ndiek, gave them food and shelter. After Clarke regained his strength, Ndiek fitted him out with some old boots and a hat and he marched back to Kisumu and stumbled into my office. It was a trying ordeal, but Clarke survived with the help of my floating piano.

Charles W Hobley, adapted from his book, KENYA From Chartered Company to Crown Colony

Tyre Trouble

In 1948, when I was eleven years old, our family set out for a holiday on the Kenya coast. Potholes, corrugations, stones and debris battered the tyres of our 1937 Chevrolet Travelall on the long, hot, dusty road from Nairobi to Mombasa. With every puncture, Dad jacked up the car, removed the faulty wheel, separated the tyre from the rim with tyre irons, extracted the tube, and pumped it up with many strokes of the Kismet foot pump to locate the leak. He scarified the rubber around the hole, and clamped on a tin pan containing solid combustible material, with the patch on the bottom. Flames and smoke spewed forth, generating heat to 'vulcanise' the patch to the tube. Many more strokes of the pump filled the tube again to be sure it didn't leak. Dad deflated the tube and stuffed it into the tyre, re-sealed the tyre to the rim with irons, pumped it up, re-attached the wheel with lug nuts, and let the jack down. Sometimes he placed a tough oval rubber 'boot' on the inside of the tyre to cover a defect bashed by a stone. My three brothers and I helped where we could.

Dad gave up after puncture number fifteen. "We'll sleep here," he said with a sigh and a frown. It was late at night and we were near the Tsavo River. We had heard stories about man-eating lions attacking workers building the railway near Tsavo. Mother and my two baby sisters spread out on the front seat and floorboards. My two younger brothers made beds in the back, enclosed with wire. Dad, my older brother and I spread our blankets on a tarpaulin on the ground.

"What are those big humps over in the bushes, Dad?" I whispered as I fixed my blanket. "I saw one move. Take a look."

"They're elephants. They like this dry country around Tsavo. They're used to cars going by. They won't hurt us. They're just feeding. See how they move slowly, stop, and move again? Hear the branches cracking? Listen carefully, and you'll hear their stomachs rumbling." I lay down under the stars, listened to the rumbles, and fell asleep.

Stan Barnett, Colorado

Target Practice

Dad and I were coming from Archer's Post and drove into Samburu park by a side road about 1959 or 1960. We were at

Buffalo Springs driving around in his old Peugeot. Suddenly there was a huge eruption, a major explosion, off to our side. My father cursed madly and sped off, saying he thought it was *shifta*. Another explosion erupted behind us. We zoomed around and lurched over the rough ground, sped round a corner and found British army vehicles and men. Dad stopped to tell them what had happened and, I guess, to warn them about the active *shifta* bandits.

The colonel was amazed to find us – actual human beings – in the car they were using for target practice! He said they had a similar car that was automated and since the park was closed to visitors they had fired at us thinking we were their target car! I guess we were very, very lucky!

Oscar Mann, Nairobi

Tapping the Wheels

A railway man due for retirement after 40 years on the Mombasa railway was presented with his long service medal and retirement present by the local DC. The DC congratulated him on his work with the railway and finally asked him, "Tell me, why do you tap the wheels of the train every time it comes into the station?" To which the railway man replied, "*Sijui bwana, hii ni desturi tu!*"

Julia Mills

Telegram Delivery in Kabarnet

Three of us, all new missionaries at Kapsabet in the 1950s, drove across the Kerio Valley on the way to Kabartonjo. Earlier we had wired Miss Baxter, our favourite Scottish language teacher (along with her broad Aberdonian accent), that we would arrive on a certain day for a week of 'brush-up' lessons before we took our required exams in the Nandi language.

We stopped at Tambach for petrol from a hand-pumped contraption that showed the petrol gurgling in and out of a glass, a gallon at a time. A local man approached our car, tenaciously holding in front of him an oilcloth-covered little parcel in the fork of a short stick. He asked for a ride to Kabarnet. We installed him in a back seat but he insisted on grasping his stick for the whole ride.

We negotiated scary hairpin bends on the descent and crossed a perilous plank bridge across the Kerio River. Our poor little car boiled over several times climbing the Tugen Hills. We poured in water. When the water was finished we searched for more. But our silent passenger just sat in the back seat holding his stick and gazing at the parcel in the fork.

At last, arriving at Kabarnet, our passenger said a gracious '*kongoi*' to us and delivered his parcel to the DC as if he was delivering the 'crown jewels.' As we drove off, we saw the DC urgently summoning us back. "This telegram is for Miss Baxter at Kabartonjo. Are you going that way?" the DC asked. We grew suspicious. A telegram for our Scottish friend, known as Jebaibai? We had sent our telegram to her days ago. But what if…We opened the telegram. It was the one we had sent!

The DC was glad to hear we were headed to Miss Baxter's. "Miss Baxter has a fee to pay for the delivery of this telegram," he said. "Would you like to pay it for her now so that I can pay this Tambach man for coming all this way to deliver your telegram." Bemused we paid the fee and drove off. We laughed as we slithered the last 19 miles on the muddy forest road. We had earlier paid to send the telegram. Now we had to deliver our own telegram and pay for its hand delivery to Kabarnet! Maybe the silent deliveryman should have paid us for transport. At least the DC had not required us to pay for the telegram's final delivery to Miss Baxter at Kabartonjo!

Lorna Eglin, Hermanus, South Africa

25 Punctures on the Way to School

Wartime rationing in the 1940s prevented our mission

station at Tenwek from getting new tyres for our 1937 Ford V8 station wagon. Bob Smith piled five of us kids – his own two children, John and Anna Verne Smith, along with me and my two sisters, Betty and Barbara Adkins – into the Ford along with our luggage for our safari to Rift Valley Academy (RVA) at Kijabe.

Most of the time we travelled to and from school by road from Tenwek (Bomet) to Lumbwa (Kipkelyon) our nearest railway station, then by train to Kijabe. But this time Bob Smith had business in Nairobi and he took us on the shorter route from Tenwek to Kijabe by way of Narok. This shorter route often made the journey much longer because of muddy roads and vehicle breakdowns.

Bob Smith had tried to replace the car's tattered tyres, but the Kericho District Commissioner refused to issue any ration permits for our mission station. We left Tenwek early that morning, the Ford sporting four badly worn tyres, with several even-more-worn-out spare tires and eight heavily patched extra inner tubes tossed on top of the luggage. That first day we stopped to mend ten punctures and only travelled 60 miles. But we did reach Narok where we spent the night with some British friends. Bob Smith, anticipating more tyre trouble, sent a telegram to RVA asking if someone could drive out to meet us with spare tyres and tubes if we didn't show up by nightfall. That day, we only progressed seven miles along the main road to Kijabe. One of the back tyres went flat five times before we could move ahead!

A British Army convoy, on manoeuvres in Maasailand, came along. Seeing our trouble, one of the drivers kindly gave us a roll of patching and a tube of cement! Late that afternoon, after more flats, it became obvious we would not get much farther that day. Bob Smith and I walked back into Narok to buy some food so we could camp beside the road. We didn't want to trouble our hosts of the night before!

We spent the night on the road. John and I stretched out as best we could on the roof rack. We listened to the howl of hyenas as we dropped off to sleep. At daybreak, we built a fire and Betty cooked oatmeal for breakfast, stirring the porridge with the only tool she could fine - a tyre iron. The oatmeal turned out gooey, so we blamed her for using a tyre iron! Later that morning, a couple of staff members arrived from RVA with extra food and – spare tyres! They helped us change the wheels and we headed for school.

Bob Smith swerved several times to keep the car in the road as he almost nodded off to sleep. By the time we reached RVA at noon, we had been on the road two-and-a-half days to travel 125 miles and mended over 25 punctures.

Bob Smith went to bed in the RVA guest room and slept straight through to the next day. Driving on into Nairobi he had five more punctures! He drove straight to the Rationing Board offices and parked at the main entrance. On finding the proper officer inside, he told his story, and walked out with permits for five new tyres! On his way home he stopped in at RVA and proudly showed us those beautiful new tyres.

Richard Adkins, USA

Lost on Mombasa Road

My father, James Donald Wroe, set out in a 1929 Chevy 6 cylinder, registration T485, from Nairobi on Sunday, June 4, 1939, headed for Moshi, Tanganyika, on what was then the main road to the coast. Employed by the Inland Revenue Department, my father expected to spend that night in Moshi with friends before departing for Voi the next day. He never arrived in Moshi.

My father had promised to wire some friends in Nairobi when he reached Voi. On Monday when his friends didn't hear from him, they became anxious. They guessed he had mistakenly taken the little-used Loitokitok road – more of a track – which was more or less deserted during this time of year. Spotter aircraft were sent in a desperate search for a man who had only carried enough food for a few days. For a week there was no news of my father. He had disappeared.

My father had indeed wandered onto the Loitokitok road and into tall elephant grass. The grass seeds clogged the radiator and the Chevy boiled and lost its water. To make matters worse he had also fractured the sump on some hard object as he drove through the tall grass. He had no choice but to carry what provisions he could and set off on foot. At night he lit a fire to keep the wild animals at bay. For five days my father wandered around in the African bush – three of those days without food or water.

On Saturday June 10th a party – only the second one since the advent of the long rains – set out from Namanga Camp under Captain Gethin on a game safari to Rhino Camp.

My father, lips swollen, completely exhausted and maybe not far from death had just been found by some Maasai. They fed my father with water one precious drop at a time though his raw sunburnt lips. Captain Gethin and his party came across my father and carried him back to Namanga as quickly as possible. There was no regular mail service from Namanga Camp but a car arrived in Nairobi on Sunday June 11th from Namanga to inform everyone that my father was safe and sound recovering in Namanga.

John Wroe, Nairobi

A Traffic Offence

I was following a car one evening in Nairobi Game Park where I was the warden. The vehicle was overflowing with a large Asian family. Suddenly one of the back doors flew open and a little girl about six years of age fell out into the dust. As the car was traveling fairly fast, I jumped out of my truck to help her thinking she must be hurt. The father soon arrived on the scene. The child was unhurt, and the gentleman was profuse in his apologies for having broken a regulation in allowing his daughter to alight from a vehicle when not at a stopping place.

Excerpted from A Warden's Diary, by Ken Beaton, 1949-50

Hitchhiking with the President's Entourage

It was 1968. I was in my last year as a student at Rift Valley Academy. During one of the school breaks my friend Dave Schaefer and I were looking for a way to break the monotony. For an adventure we decided to travel from Kijabe to Nakuru to visit Steve Kellogg, a fellow student who was home with his parents during the vacation. We hiked five miles out to the Nairobi-Nakuru road that wound down the escarpment and stood beside the road and stuck out our thumbs in the classic hitchhiker pose. After only a few minutes a formation of motorcycles swept by. Recognizing them as the forerunners of the President's motorcade, we stepped back quickly and stood respectfully as the motorcycles and official limousines carrying His Excellency, the President Mzee Jomo Kenyatta, and his entourage swept past with flags flying. We waited several minutes and then stepped forward with our thumbs out to try again. Before long an expensive looking black car came speeding toward us. To our surprise it slowed and stopped. The man in the car asked where we were going. When we told him our destination he invited us to climb in, and we settled into the soft seats. As we chatted, we discovered he was a minister in the government. He was part of the presidential party but had arrived late. Now he was hurrying to catch up with the others. By this time, we were hurtling down the road at great speed, confident that all other traffic had been pulled aside, and we soon caught up with the other cars.

Now our pace slowed from time to time as the President's car paused frequently to allow him and the rest of his entourage to wave and greet the people assembled at various stops. We waved too. I wonder what the people thought about the two teen-aged wazungu who were part of the President's party that day! In very short order, we arrived in Nakuru. Our kind benefactor let us off at the traffic circle and we made our way to the Kelloggs' for a fun weekend.

Monday morning we set out to hitchhike back to Kijabe. We walked for miles. Car after car passed us by without even slowing down. After over an hour, a car pulled over. It was a missionary family who recognized us and stopped to give us a ride. The back seat was already filled with their children, but they squeezed over to make room for us as we piled in, matatu style. We were thankful for the ride, but it was a good lesson on the varying fortunes of the hitchhiker.

Cam Arensen, Abu Dhabi

Mid-lake Collision

Between 1967 and 1974 I lived around the shores of Lake Victoria in Mwanza, Bukoba and Kisumu and travelled frequently on the *Victoria* and the *Usoga*. But it was in Bukoba that these great ships became a significant part of our social life. On Thursday evenings, the *Victoria* would arrive from Mwanza, and the *wazungu* community of the town would descend on the wharf and swarm up the gang plank to the 1st class saloon to "go out for dinner." Other than the sad draughty barn of the "Lake Hotel" dining room, there was really nowhere else to partake of this bit of bourgeois pleasure, and on the *Victoria* we sat at linen table cloths and partook of minestrone soup, roast lamb and sponge pudding, served on EARH embossed plates, and shovelled down with silver plated cutlery. We would consume quantities of Tusker, and engage dear "Sooty" the captain in conversation, helping him continue his Tusker flow, which had started at breakfast.

Sooty was a real character of that huge inland sea, as was "Dirty George" who captained the *Usoga*. DG was a Liverpudlian, swarthy, with a fine line in Liverpudlian language to berate his crew. It was quite in character that the neater Sooty captained the elegant *Victoria* and DG the bustling, work-a-day *Usoga*.

There is a story, perhaps apocryphal, that one clear, calm moonlit night, the *Victoria* was steaming west-east across the Lake, and the *Usoga* north-south, both captained by hopelessly inebriated captains (their 1st officers were the real unsung heros), and they collided, right in the middle of that large lake. There were no other ships on the lake at the time.

Another more likely story is that the *Usoga* was going to be called the *Busoga*, but the porters carrying the bits up to Kisumu (Port Florence) lost the letter B.

Tony Moody, Australia

Rhino on the Runway

My brother, Keith Cairns, flew a small Luscombe Silvair from Nairobi to Pretoria in 1962. Here are some excerpts from his diary:

"I bought the little Luscombe Silvair for 800 pounds in East African currency with the idea to get my hours up for my licence. I had failed to obtain a commercial licence owing to colour blindness. I flew it all over Kenya, but still needed more hours, so I decided to do the trip to Pretoria and back…I knew I did not have the range between some landing spots, so I installed a hand wobble pump behind the back seat. When I was getting low on fuel, I would open a four-gallon tin of petrol and pump it to the tank while I was flying. The smell of petrol was strong. How it never caught fire I do not know. I carried three of these cans. I know the Department of Aviation would have grounded me had they known.

"Mom took me to the Airport when a commercial pilot came up to me and asked where the hell was I going. When told, he said, in front of Mum, he would not even get in and take it to the end of the runway!

"The plane had been taken over by the military during the war. At the end, it ended up in a scrap metal dump, where somebody bought it and hung it up in a tree for the kids to play with. It was then returned to the dump where Keith Campling bought it, worked on it and got I licensed. He used it to take people up for joy rides.

"On flying down to Mombasa I had a very strong head wind, and was getting short of petrol, so I landed at Voi and refuelled. On taking off I was just about airborne when a rhino came across the runway. I just missed it. (p.s. I had to change my jocks)."

Daphne Johnson, Herefordshire, UK

Motorcycle Menace

My mother first came to Kenya in 1919 when my father lived at Sergoit. They used ox carts for transport and a shopping expedition to Eldoret took three days – one for getting there, one for shopping and one for getting home.

An up-to-date neighbour had a motorcycle and one day offered my mother a speedier journey into town. The track was a bit rough and when the motorcycle went over a particularly bad bump, my mother flew into the air and landed beside the road. The motorcyclist, presumably concentrating on the ups and downs, did not notice for some time that he'd lost his passenger. After several miles he eventually turned back and found my mother sitting disconsolately by the roadside.

My father, no doubt inspired by his progressive neighbour, later acquired his own motorcycle. My mother had lost her enthusiasm for pillion riding so my father added a sidecar. It seems motorcycles resented my mother's presence in some way because on one of their trips in the side car a wheel came off and my mother, with a baby this time, was once again deposited onto the road.

Kathy Forrester, adapted from **Trans-Nzoia Scrap Book**

A Train Journey

In 1948 I accompanied my mother from Mombasa to Nairobi by train. I had just returned to Kenya, the land of my birth, after spending a year in various places overseas and it was such a pleasure to get home.

Back then, the train left the Station on Mombasa Island in the late afternoon. We did not share a first class compartment but had adjoining compartments to ourselves. The carriage attendant arranged for bedding on payment of a tiny fee and off we went.

By dusk we had climbed out of the steamy heat of Mombasa and were trundling along about 50 miles from our starting point when we were called for dinner by a waiter walking along the corridor of each carriage playing a tune on a very small sort of xylophone.

In the dining car the immaculate starched white tablecloth together with equally clean napkins for each place were cheerful and welcoming. My mother and I were seated at a table for four and the other two travellers were a young Mzungu and a very large elderly gentleman with a huge bushy beard.

The young man said the first time he had taken the train from Mombasa, the journey to Nairobi took several hours longer than the present journey was scheduled to take. My mother, who had arrived in Kenya in 1922, was a person who often liked to trump another person's story if at all possible. She promptly stated that the first time she had undertaken the journey from Mombasa there were no corridors in the passenger coaches and each compartment was fully equipped with its own toilet facilities. There was no dining car either. The train stopped at Voi where dinner was served in what was called a Dak Bungalow at the station. The following morning, the train stopped at Sultan Hamud where breakfast was served also at the station.

Not to be outdone, the elderly gentleman announced in a rather strange eastern European accent, "The first time I travelled from Mombasa, we walked!"

I later discovered the elderly gentleman was Vladamir Verbi who, after resigning from the Missionary Society to which he belonged, bought a small parcel of land at Wundanyi in the Taita Hills where he built his home. In 1939 he became quite famous after being tried (and acquitted) in Court for shooting his mother-in-law apparently in the mistaken belief that she was a crow that was part of a flock damaging his garden. When I last visited Wundanyi, his house had become a school and his grave was somewhat overgrown but still visible in the garden.

Michael Aronson, Nairobi

Hiding the Evidence

I was lucky to be brought up in the world of aviation in Kenya, as my father was an aviation pioneer. I recall flying to the coast as a five-year-old in a Miles Gemini. We landed on the beach in front of the Nyali Beach Hotel and I helped pulled the aircraft into the coconut palms so the tide didn't wash it away. We often spent school holidays at the hangar in Nairobi West (now Wilson Airport) trying to scrounge a ride. My biggest problem was getting terribly airsick when I flew. Once my father made a trip to the Kinangop in a Tiger Moth. He asked my younger bro and I to come along for the ride. We strapped ourselves into the front open cockpit and departed. The outward journey was fine. But I began to feel sick as we returned. I knew if I let go of my lunch overboard, my father would receive it in the rear cockpit. He didn't take lightly to wimp kids. I informed my little brother that I was going to deposit my lunch into my plimsolls that I was taking off. I gave him strict instructions that on arrival at Nairobi West he had to attract my father's attention while I dumped out the evidence behind the hangar. I told him he'd face certain death if he informed my father.

Chris Noon

Alone in the Desert

Our safari company tried out a new route from the southeastern end of Lake Turkana to Marsabit National Park through the Koroli Desert. We were halfway across the 30 mile sandy stretch of the Koroli Desert, and the driver had not seen another vehicle all morning and there was only one set of tire tracks in the sand. In the heat haze ahead he saw a typical mirage, which seemed to change from a small black stone into a black boulder. On approaching the object, it turned into an elderly American lady in a blue safari suit, sitting in the sand alone in the middle of the inhabited, scorching hot desert. She arose as our vehicle pulled up beside her and inquired most politely, without showing any sign of relief or pleasure, "Excuse me, but would you be going anywhere near Mar-say-bit." Had we not decided to take that route, she probably wouldn't have seen another vehicle for a week and faced a horrible death from thirst. Obviously this good lady had not the faintest idea of the danger of her situation. She was one of a group of six safari clients in a Volkswagen Combi that had stopped for a pee on their way to Marsabit Lodge. The car had accidentally driven off without her some three hours previously and nobody had missed her! We eventually got through to Nairobi from Marsabit, and told her tour company we'd picked up their guest in the desert. They sent an aeroplane up for her as there was still no sign of her VW Combi.

Dick Hedges, Nairobi

'Tight' Fanbelt

My mother, Edith Averill Vail, was heading to Timboroa in her Morris Minor when the fan belt broke. She pulled to the side of the road. An Afrikaner stopped and asked if he could help. She opened the bonnet and leaned in to have a look. When he noted the problem he commanded her, "Take your tights off!" My mother was horrified and worried about the man's intentions, but she complied. He tied her tights together and fastened them around the pulleys as a makeshift fan belt and she went on her way.

Mary McLean, Langata

Motorbike Overboard!

When I was up near the Kafu River, I wanted to go to Masindi to get some stores. I got to a crossing at the river, which was about twenty yards wide, and found only one very small canoe there. There were any amount of crocodiles in the river, and the canoe was only capable of carrying two natives and about two loads each trip, so it took a considerable time to get all my safari across…The motorbicycle was last to go over, and I foolishly stood it up in the canoe, telling one of the boys to hold it. They had got to about the middle of the stream, when to my dismay the thing suddenly wobbled and the canoe turned turtle. I hurriedly took a gun from Kadoli and started to fire into the water fairly near the two natives who were clinging to the canoe, the idea being, of course, to keep the crocodiles away from them. All the natives on both sides of the river thought I had gone quite mad and was trying to kill the two boys for sinking my motorbike. The boys on the far side were shouting to the ones on my side to stop me and the ones on my side explained that they could not do anything or I might start on them as well. I told Kadoli what the idea was, and he managed to quieten them. Meanwhile the canoe with the two boys had floated downstream, and they landed on my side of the river.

The problem then was how to get my motorbike out of the river. I sent a boy off to a nearby village for as much rope as he could find, and luckily he brought back quite a good length. I then offered five rupees to anyone who would get into the river and tie one end of the rope to the bicycle, but there was nothing doing. None of them knew how to swim, and at any rate, they asked, who would go underneath the water to be eaten by crocodiles?

There was nothing for it but to do my own dirty work, so taking the rope, a longish pole, and a rifle into the canoe with me, and one boy to paddle, I pushed out into the middle of the stream. When I got to the spot where the bike had gone down, I started to feel about with the pole until I touched it, then I stuck the pole deep into the mud of the river bottom and told the boy to hold onto it. I was already stripped except for my helmet, and after firing about twenty rounds out of the .303 up and downstream and all around the canoe, I went overboard holding onto the pole and taking one end of the rope, fashioned into a noose, with me. It was a most unpleasant job, and I expected at any moment to feel a croc's jaws round me. I got down as quickly as I could, felt along the motorcycle until I found the saddle, then slipped the noose round it, and came up much quicker than I had gone down. We rowed back, paying out the rope behind us, and then the boys hauled in the motorcycle. I drained and refilled the sump and petrol tank, and to my joy the little Douglas started up almost immediately, seeming none the worse for its immersion.

*Hugh Foster in the book **Uganda Adventures** published by his son Francis Foster*

Biking from Kaptagat to Turi

On one of my school holidays during my first year at Prince of Wales school about 1941, I wanted to visit friends at Kaptagat. I was 12 and the school had just returned to Nairobi from Naivasha where it had moved to at the outbreak of World War 2. The war was still on and we had rationing on petrol as well as bread, butter and meat.

I had previously studied at Kaptagat School, which Zoe Foster had founded so her children, Robert, Francis and Mary could be educated. I planned to spend half the holiday at Kaptagat and then Robert and Francis would come to my parents' farm at Turi. We suggested we cycle the eighty miles from Kaptagat to Turi to save on petrol. Robert was a year younger than me and Francis was a year younger. So, aged 12, 11 and about 9, we planned to travel the 80 miles on our own with basic bicycles without gears.

We practiced by riding from Kaptagat to Eldoret and back, some 20 miles each way, in a day. We encountered a hailstorm. The vicious hailstones stung painfully and even hiding under our cycles didn't help.

We prepared for the journey to Turi. We wore khaki shorts and short-sleeved shirts and only tackies (tennis shoes) on our feet. We took with us spare shirts and shorts, a raincoat, a hat, and each of us had a ground sheet or blanket. We had no tent, but we did have our trusty sheath knives. We carried a tin of corned beef, a tin of peaches, a tin of sweetened condensed milk (to us, as young boys, this was the most important item of all), bottles of water, a few sandwiches and an apple or two together with tubes of Wine Gums to suck on the way.

We set off over the corrugated and extremely dusty road. When we started the long ascent up to Timboroa, we felt the strain. We saw a large tree alongside the road and decided to a rest and eat under the tree's shade. Safari ants attacked us so we sped off. The road became very slippery and wet from rain as we neared Timboroa. We made it to the dam close to Timboroa and found the pump house used by the steam locomotives. At 9000 feet elevation it was very cold. We ate what food we had and settled down for the night in the warmth of the wood-fired steam pump engine. The pump attendant left us alone after our initial greetings. We suffered through the most uncomfortable night I can remember. We had no sleeping bags, just a small ground sheet or blanket each, a raincoat to cover us, a piece of wood covered with an item of clothing (mine was my shirt) as a pillow and a concrete floor as our bed.

The next morning we set off early, descending along slippery roads through forests damp from previous rain to Mau Summit then Molo and ultimately Turi. My mother was very pleased to see us. I wonder now if our parents had any qualms about us cycling that distance alone.

Michael Rutherford, Surrey, UK

Pigs in the Rolls

Horst von Kaufman emigrated from Germany to Tanganyika in 1935. In 1944 he worked for Captain H M 'Black' Harries at his Solai farm. Horst bought his own farm in the area ten years later. Among other interests, he started pig farming and would deliver his pigs to the Nakuru railway station using a 1926 Rolls Royce that had been converted into a pick-up truck!

Taken from Coastweek

Car Wreck

One time my father was working on the elephant project in Tsavo and had been there for some time. My mom planned to drive down together with me and Iki (my sister) and my best friend Johnny Rozsa. We left early in the morning and drove for what seemed forever. Iki was sleeping in front and we were somewhere near Kibwezi, I think, when the car skidded and went over the edge of the built-up road and turned over a few times on the way down, landing with a great thud on its wheels. None of us was hurt, though we were badly shaken. Iki woke up and said something like, "I just had a strange dream. Why did you wake me?"

Since the car was on its wheels and seemed OK, except for a crushed roof and broken windscreen, we decided we had better just go on. Dad was expecting us and might worry we'd had an accident or something!

We drove through the park with a guide and came to the banks of the Tsavo River. Dad's camp was on the other side. Seeing us, he waded across and came right up to the car. "Why are you so late?" he shouted.

My mom, amazed that he didn't notice the extremely obvious state of the car, didn't say anything for a while! Eventually she said, "Have a look at the car." She had to say it a few times before my dad relaxed his tirade and had a look.

His jaws flew open and his eyes boggled! "My God! What happened to you?"

My mom told our story, including the funny bit about Iki's dream. We all got out and waded across the fast-flowing, fairly deep brown river with him and a gang of workers, who carried all our bags. It was nice to be out of the car and alive!

Oscar Mann, Nairobi

Open Air Shower

My Father was a hunter in Kenya. One day while driving in the bush a white man came rushing out towards the vehicle frantically waving his arms. Dad stopped the Land Rover and asked if everything was ok to which the man replied, "If you wouldn't mind turning round, my wife is taking a shower under those trees!!"

Franca Ross

Maasai Man Points the Way

We'd mistaken a cattle path for a road, and it was getting less passable by the minute when we came across a Maasai, and asked him where this road went. His utter disbelief at our blind stupidity was inescapable as he answered by gesturing clearly in the direction our Land Rover was pointed.

Joe Weinstein

Lions on the Road

Back in the 1930s my grandfather was driving back to the farm from Kitale late one night when he came upon a pride of lions in the road. He stopped and the car stalled. He was driving a Model T Ford, which was started by a hand crank, so he had to get out, walk to the front of the car and start the car in front of the lions before he could continue his journey home.

Mike Bacon

A Walk on the Wild Side

I took my first holiday abroad to Kenya in March 1966

where I had two brothers farming in the highlands. Jim and Geoff met me at the airport and took me to their farm in the Trans-Nzoia district. Jim suggested he and I should go on safari to the Serengeti Game Reserve.

We set off in a Volkswagen Variant Hatchback. At the park entrance a Park Ranger assured us the road was *mzuri* and the long rains hadn't started. We passed through a half dozen or so shallow riverbeds, all dry. But as we rounded a sharp bend with scrub on both sides, we suddenly landed the car in the middle of a flash flood with water filling the riverbed. We scrambled out of the car onto the riverbank. Not wanting to wait until the water subsided we decided to push the car to the gentle slope on the other side and with the assistance of slight vehicle buoyancy, we achieved our aim.

"Light me a cigarette, quickly!" I yelled. I wasn't even a smoker. Looking down we found leeches clinging to our skin. We forgot our modesty and stripped down and with trembling fingers detached the ugly bloodsuckers.

Darkness fell rapidly and we tried in vain to fire life back into our saturated vehicle. We eventually retreated into the car as our refuge for the night. Dawn broke, and we still couldn't get the car started. I remembered having seen a road works tractor some way back on the track we'd covered the day before. Jim decided to risk the walk back. With a feeling of utter helplessness and terrifying loneliness I watched as Jim vanished briskly into the horizon. I slapped and wondered just how many mosquitoes had shared our sleeping quarters during the night.

My watch showed 6:30 am and I occupied myself with calculations on the dust covered car bonnet. If the tractor was six miles away and Jim walked at four miles per hour, how long… my mind dismissed the possibility Jim would never return, even when a spotted hyena appeared from nowhere, eyed me inquisitively and slunk off.

Every few restless minutes I strolled aimlessly 20 or 30 yards along the track to gaze through the tall elephant grass into the seemingly endless treeless plain. There was an eerie stillness. Four hours had passed since Jim had set forth in search of the mythical tractor.

Finally through the heat haze and salty perspiration burning my eyes, I saw on the horizon a tiny bluebottle-like speck with a dust trail. Soon Jim plunged the tractor into the water-filled drift – which had abated quite a bit overnight – and halted next to the car shouting, "It's got a tow rope."

Simultaneously a lorry full of workers arrived from the direction of Seronera Game Lodge. With unanimous unwillingness to alight from their vehicle, they gesticulated wildly and shouted some words, which I did not understand at the time: *"Simba! Simba! Hatari!"*

I stood rooted to the ground, my legs turning to jelly as not more than 20 feet away from the edge of the road a huge lion and three lionesses stood up in the tall grass and ambled off.

With a short tow the car roared to life. All these years later I still get shivers when I think of that perilous walk on the wild side.

Fred Faulkner, Northern Ireland

Stranded at Stony Athi

About February 1942 I returned from a lovely holiday with Lance and Martha Bonar in Malindi. I had my six-month-old baby Guy, and we shared a compartment with a Mrs Trench, whom I'd never met before. It was one of the horsebox compartments without a corridor. We had to get out at one station for breakfast in the dining car, have our breakfast, and then return to our compartment at the next station. We reached Stony Athi and I was helped out and onto the platform as the train stopped. However, it immediately began to move again, and I raced along after it, holding my baby on one hip and tin of Cow-and-gate milk powder in my other hand. I watched the train gather speed and disappear down the track, with the sympathetic young Indian stationmaster unable to do anything. Stony Athi was, in fact, then only a train siding for loading cattle, without even a proper track to get to it! The only communication was to the next station, Athi River.

The stationmaster duly took us to his own quarters and produced a lot of hard-boiled eggs and a pot of tea. Lucky I had the milk powder for the baby!

We waited until 4 pm when another train arrived and we duly boarded it. But as the train gathered speed, I spotted my husband Rupert charging across the plains to Stony Athi in his pickup to find us, having had a message, I suppose from Mrs Trench in Nairobi! I signalled frantically from the window. Luckily he saw me and we were reunited at Athi River.

Helen Hallowes, Pietermaritzburg, South Africa

Forgotten

Paul and Signa Worthley were family friends and great with us kids as they included us and treated us like adults. Paul had been an officer in Tanks and Signa was Swedish. Paul used to suffer from what was known as shell shock. When they lived in Uganda they went out to see friends and on the way the car got stuck in the mud. Signa got out to push and managed to free the car from the mire. Paul drove on and arrived at his destination. His hosts asked, "Where is Signa?" Paul had to rush back. He had forgotten all about Signa after she had pushed him out of the mud.

Andrew Cobb, Durban

Motorcycles on the Escarpment

Mick and I were firm friends, both born in the Rift Valley, schooled at the Prince of Wales, Kabete, and joining the Kenya Police on the same day in 1946 and both owning old motorcycles. This inevitably led to adventure.

Both our parents were still active – Mick's at Gilgil and mine at Lake Farm, Nakuru. When our respective duties permitted, the pair of us would roar down the escarpment at dawn on our motorcycles. At Gilgil Mick would take the west road home and I continued to the Lanet turnoff. We'd rendezvous in the late afternoon of the next day and head back to Nairobi along the same route, our motorcycle panniers loaded with our kitbags and home produce.

We took the potential road hazards in our stride. These ranged from swarms of bees (and we always wore khaki shorts and open necked shirts) to the wild antics of the overloaded and competitively racing 'Banana Express' buses.

One evening after speedily overtaking a Banana Express we were surprised by all the cat calls from the 'tunniboi' and passengers and the frantic hooting by the driver. As we ascended the escarpment out of the Rift Valley this unusually enthusiastic and noisy vehicle continued to pursue us closely, but we soon left it behind on the steep climb. Descending through Limuru towards Nairobi, we sped along, Mick on his old BSA side valve and me on an old ex-army Matchless. We noticed the same bus catching up. Passengers were hanging out of the windows and the driver was still hooting at us.

We decided this fellow needed at the very least a sharp lecture on road safety and bus speed limits, so we stopped. The bus, belching clouds of steam from the radiator, skidded to a halt behind us and out jumped an elderly African gentleman. Clutching his battered hat to his chest his 'Turn Boy' joined him

carrying a large bag – which had fallen off Mick's b[...]
the bottom of the escarpment! For once neither M[...]
much to say except, "Asante sana!"

J Brian Boulton, Wes[...]

Brake Test in Sudan

We entered Sudan by road through Lokichoggio in the late 1970s and had to drive all the way to Juba to clear customs and license my well-used Toyota Land Cruiser. The paperwork took two weeks and meanwhile we camped under some mango trees near the Nile River. To be registered, the Toyota had to pass a unique road test. To test the brakes one had to drive toward a tree at forty miles per hour. At the last crucial second the police inspector would drop his arm and the driver hit the brakes. If the brakes worked well, the vehicle slid to a stop before hitting the tree. If the brakes did not work, the vehicle collided with the tree and failed the test. The tree had many gashes from former failures. The brakes on the old Toyota were not that good, but since my friend John Pelletier had previously owned the Toyota, he knew how to get the most out of them. We designated him as the driver for the test. Just before he started the dash toward the tree, he pumped the brake pedal over and over, building up hydraulic pressure. He raced toward the tree and when he got the signal to stop, he stood on the brake with all the power of his right leg. The brakes grabbed and he stopped within inches of the tree. My Toyota passed inspection and was duly registered with a new Sudanese license plate.

From Jon Arensen's book, **Drinking the Wind**

Aeroplane Tales

Here are two amusing incidents going back to the old days of East African Airways and the Embakasi Airport.

y wife and I and two small children arrived at Embakasi catch a Viscount prop plane for a 24-hour flight to London, refuelling in North Africa. I didn't have the key to open the boot of our Humber Super Snipe to get at our luggage. I tried prising open the boot, first with a screwdriver and later a tyre lever loaned by fellow passengers. Eventually the back of the car looked like a butterfly with wings half extended, but I still couldn't pull out the suitcases. I returned to Langata for the spare key and arrived back at the airport to hear the flight was just boarding. I hastily left the car to be collected by the driver, while my wife, two children and I ignored customs and rushed across the runway and climbed the mobile boarding staircase onto the thirty-seater narrow-bodied Viscount. As the seatbelt sign went out, my wife, sitting some seats ahead of me, turned to a friendly Singh alongside her and inquired what time the flight would land in London. He told her the flight was going to Sarajevo, not London!

In the second story, I was flying on my own from Nairobi to the Berlin trade fair in one of the early Jumbos. We had just lined up for take-off behind a Pan-Am plane going south, when a crying, screaming sound erupted from the rear of the aircraft. Most passengers thought somebody was having an epileptic fit. The aircraft did a U-turn and taxied back to the airport buildings. A mature American lady disembarked, escorted by the cabin crew, to wait for her baggage from the hold. She was still sobbing. Later we heard the full details of what had happened. The mature American lady in question had decided after boarding the plane that she could not bear the thought of leaving her safari driver with whom she had fallen madly in love. She insisted she be returned to the arms of this young man and become his third wife. She would not take no for an answer from the cabin crew, and informed them that if she could not disembark to be reunited with her lover, she would scream all the way to London!

Dick Hedges, Nairobi

Hospitality Kenya-style

I lived in Kenya from 1957 and after passing my GCE my parents bought me a Honda 125 licence plate KJD 52. I started working in Nairobi with an airline and as my then-girlfriend lived in Mombasa I used to ride my Honda from Nairobi to Mombasa twice monthly. In those days the road was tarmac only from Voi to Mombasa – the rest of the road was dirt and sand. One day I left Nairobi after breakfast and started my trip to the coast. After Mtito Andei the engine stopped running and I knew I had sand in the piston. It was dark with no lights to be seen. The sounds of animals made me nervous. Suddenly out of nowhere three Maasai stood next to me and I told them, "*Pikipiki yangu imeharibika.* My motorcycle has broken down." They looked at me and the eldest told the others, "*Sukuma,*" and they pushed my bike and me into the bush. After about half an hour we came to an area of a few huts and a warm fire. They offered me water, food and a place to sleep. I didn't close my eyes, but I did have a rest. The next morning the eldest offered me warm *damu* from the cows. I said, "*Asante sana,*" but felt I would be sick any minute. They pushed my bike and me to the nearby railway line where I waited for a freight train to pass. I stood on the rail tracks and waved. The engine slowed down and the train driver, a Singh, came down, and helped me lift my motorcycle onto a coach. I boarded as well and finally arrived in Mombasa after a long trip. My bike got new piston rings and after three days I drove back to Nairobi, stopping at my new friends' place, giving some sweets to the kids and thanking the Maasai once again.

Twenty years later I took my family on vacation from Germany to Mombasa and we rented a car and drove from Mombasa to Nairobi. I stopped and looked for my old friends. After searching for a few hours I found the place, which had become a small village. A man greeted me and said, "Jambo Bwana Andreas. Karibu." After twenty years! He even showed me a paper where I had written my address, which he had kept all these years. Tears ran down my cheeks.

Andreas Reichmanis, Buechenbeuren, Germany

Unbelievable Tales

Higgs and the Geita Night-Rider

In late 1951 James Penhaligon, born of Cornish parents, was taken at six months old to live on the remote Geita gold mine in Tanganyika. With both parents working, he was cared for by an African ayah. Through her, and several African children, not least Lutoli, he became fluent in Swahili before he ever spoke English. To his African friends James, who they loved as one of their own, was known as Jimu.

In Geita there was a motley collection of people from different countries and backgrounds. It made for many amusing anecdotes. The excerpt below describes an incident in which 'Higginson,' ex British-Indian army colonel, now Geita askari-chief, has a most unusual night-time encounter.

In 1958 an event happens in Geita, so curious that its fame in local folklore is guaranteed. The drunken outcasts, Higgs and Heathfield, lurch out from the club into the parking area. They're even drunker than usual. Higgs finds his motorbike and pulls it off its stand. He straddles it and kick-starts the engine. Heathfield has disappeared, and Higgs calls for him impatiently, the bike's gear engaged and clutch held in. He feels a weight alight, Heathfield's warm body against his back, moist breath on the nape of his neck. He *does* get too clutchy, and more than a bit pathetic, after ten quarts of Whitecap. Higgs is used to it. He burps, lets out the clutch with his left hand, and rolls up the revs with his right. The big Harley Davidson roars, and the twosome ride unsteadily away, up the gravelled road in the direction of their homes.

Now Heathfield *really* starts to exceed himself. At first Higgs feels his passenger's arms move up from around the hips, to grasp his shoulders. "What the hell are you playing at?" he shouts above the roar of the engine. No answer. Now Heathfield's nails dig deeply into Higgs's shoulders. The pain is excruciating.

"Stop it, you damnable fool!" Higgs yells, but the nails dig deeper, and begin to scratch painfully down his back. The agony is so extreme that Higgs, rounding a corner, loses control, and the bike plummets off the road into dense undergrowth.

Higgs hears his bike hitting something. He finds himself on a bed of soft branches, and suddenly feels very inebriated. To hell with it, he thinks, and falls asleep. His last thoughts are, "Where the hell is Heathfield?" and "I'm not taking *him* home again."

At seven in the morning Higgs awakes to searing tropical sunshine, the buzzing of myriad insects, and a skimpy memory of the previous night. When he tries to rise, he finds his back and shoulders are in agony. Gingerly he feels the scratches on his back, to discover half-inch deep lacerations running from shoulder-tip to waistline. He limps to where his bike lies on its side by the trunk of a *Mbuia* tree, and is astonished to see the near side of the petrol tank has four deep dents. He pulls the bike up, and finds the same on the other side. One of the dents has a hole in it. Protruding from the hole is a very large, bloodstained claw-nail. Higgs's clingy passenger of last night was not Heathfield. Heathfield had never made it to the motorbike. On staggering into the fresh air from the club, Heathfield had felt awfully tired, seen an inviting flowerbed and collapsed into it.

Higgs's passenger was a full-grown leopard! The news spreads like bush-fire. Some *Wazungus* say he's making this up. Whites who marry blacks are probably liars, and worse. But how can they explain his lacerations and the holes in the petrol tank? The claw? Why does Heathfield admit sleeping in a flower bed? Higgs brought him to the club, and the bike was undamaged then. Did Higgs sneak out between drinks, disable and puncture his own bike's tank, insert a leopard claw into the hole, severely lacerate himself, then sidle back in and act normally? Wouldn't someone have noticed the blood? And how did he get rid of Heathfield on the road? Unless he and Heathfield are in this together. But *why?* Why would these men, no matter their individual faults, play a prank like this? It doesn't make sense.

Three days after the incident, while Higgs is still receiving daily injections and dressings for his wounds, a leopard is shot just two miles from the club by Marcello Barelli, Antonio's father and our great white hunter. His rear right foot is missing a claw, and the toe-pad is torn and septic. When his back feet are placed against the fuel tank, the claw positions match the punctures. The incident is closed. The leopard weighs two hundred pounds, and is fully nine foot from nose to tail. He will be remembered for years as the Geita 'Night-Rider,' who hitched a lift with the constabulary. When Higgs recovers his limited dignity, he's often heard to brag, after several Whitecaps, "I gave that sod a lift for half a bloody mile!" The legend of *Higgs and the Night-Rider* takes flight, and soon is heard as far afield as Dar es Salaam, Iringa and Morogoro.

From James Penhaligon's book **Speak Swahili Dammit**

Flying Teeth

My father and I went on a bird-hunting trip near Meru around 1970. We brought Gulam Hussein Habib – a real comedian – along to do the slaughtering properly since my mother was a Muslim. He also did our cooking. If we wanted him to cook well, we gave him a tot of brandy. This one night we'd given him too much brandy and Gulam got drunk. When we brought the birds we'd shot so he could slaughter them, he was as likely to cut off the legs as the head. We decided to drive home. As we neared our home in Meru, Gulam's speech became very slurred. I assumed it was his drunkenness. When we got him home, his face looked very shrunken around the mouth. "What's wrong with your face?" I asked.

He felt his mouth and shouted, "Oh no! I've lost my

dentures!" He had thrown up several times on the trip home and we realized he must have lost the dentures during one of his vomiting episodes. Since he'd gotten the expensive dentures from his son, a dentist, Gulam insisted we go back and find them. We remembered the places we'd stopped the car so Gulam could throw up, so we went back and sure enough found the dentures. Once he'd retrieved his false teeth, I refused to let him bring the teeth into the car. I had a new Land Rover and didn't want his filthy dentures smelling it up. He solved the problem by tying a string to the dentures and dangling them out the window. As we drove along, the teeth whipped back and forth in the wind. We drove past a bicyclist and the flying teeth rapped him on the head and knocked him off his bicycle. We stopped and took the man to the nearest police station and told the policeman what had happened.

When the policeman heard our story of the dentures hitting the man on the bike, he became angry with us and asked, "Do you think I'm stupid?" He finally called the OCS, a man whom we knew. The OCS settled everything down and told us to pay to fix the bicycle's bent rim and sent us home.

Satish Wason, Timau

Between the Legs of a Giraffe

My unbelievable story started out with my acquisition of a PV Volvo while my wife, Miriam, and I worked in Kenya in the early 1970s.

The PV had a very distinctive appearance with a snub-nosed bonnet, split windscreen and a long swept back body, rather like the American gangster-era cars. It was built to cope with the harsh back roads of Scandinavia in winter and was very tough indeed. The engine was raised high above a girder axle, truck style. The front wheels had small twin shock absorbers either side of the coil springs and she handled beautifully. In East Africa the car gained great fame when Joginder Singh drove a PV Volvo to victory in the East African Safari Rally in 1965, the first time the race was won by a non-mzungu. Only a few PVs were brought into Kenya, mainly for rallying. I was lucky enough to acquire one.

I had been driving a Saab Sports but had recently written it off in a crash with a tea lorry in the Kericho area. So, I was in the market for another car. It was love at first sight when my squash partner, Bir Singh, a mechanic with Kakamega Motors, turned up for our weekly squash session at Kakamega Club in a light blue PV Volvo. I'd never seen the likes of a car like that before, but instantly desired it. After the squash we usually cooled off with a Tusker beer in the Sports Club bar. I asked him about this new car of his, which was actually 20 years old. He explained he had bought it for £150 from an Irish priest who was leaving Kenya. I told him how much I liked it and next week offered him £175 for the car. No way, he liked it too much. Well, each week I raised my offer by £25 and when the price reached £225 he crumbled. I loved that car, the great sweeping back, the long gear stick and fluid gear change, strong engine and tough body. It was left-hand drive, but in the sparse traffic conditions of the time that was no problem at all. I immediately bought some car paint and changed her livery. For most of the body I chose British Racing Green. The bonnet I painted matt black with blackboard paint for no-glare night driving. Then the roof and boot I did a nice cream. There was no mistaking my Volvo. There was nothing else on Kenya's roads remotely like it.

After two or three local weekend safaris, school holidays came round and we decided to visit Mombasa and the Kenya Coast. We loaded up our camping gear and set off down the escarpment to Kisumu to drive across the Rift Valley to Nairobi. The Leach family in Lower Kabete, Nairobi had befriended us, so we used to stay with them when we passed through the Kenyan capital. James and Helen were long-term expats working with the Ministry of Overseas Development with experience working in several African countries including Botswana and Nigeria. They were great hosts and board-game players. With three young children Tom, Bengie, and Rachel, each evening ended with an enthusiastically played board game.

We set off early next morning for the different sort of drive down to Mombasa, crossing the Athi Plains to the lovely watering hole of Hunter's lodge, sweeping by the volcanic chain of the Chyulu Hills followed by the long hot drive through the magnificent scenery of Tsavo Game Park. As we neared the Coast the vegetation became tropical, coconut palms abounded, and brightly dressed chocolate-brown people replaced the darker people of the interior. The sun was going down and the air became permeated with interesting smells, some richly sweet, others resonating strongly of roast potatoes. The Kenya Coast announced itself in many magical ways.

We used to camp at a small resort called White Sands, just North of Mombasa. It was a fun place and camping under the coconut palms to the sound of the Indian Ocean breakers crashing on the distant reef was a blissful experience. The white sandy beaches and easy-entry sea temperatures made beach idling a delightful way to spend the days. A series of ever-welcoming hotels dotted the coastline and made for interesting architectural and gourmet dining explorations. It was wonderful to wander round Mombasa Old Town in carefree flip flops, ducking into attractive cool drinks places for fresh pineapple juice, or swigging coconut milk from a newly chopped nut from a street vendor. The heat made for slow languid living. One day we drove North and took the ferry across Kilifi Creek. Nobody showed impatience as we waited 30 minutes for the ferry to slowly make its way back over to our side. We propped ourselves up on the quayside with newspaper cones of roast groundnuts to munch as we chatted away and watched the world go by. We drove along the coast road to Malindi, stopping at Gede to browse around a long deserted ruined Arab town. We knew the coast had a long history of interaction between natives and Arabs, creating a largely Muslim Swahili-speaking culture that seemed quite divorced from the rest of Kenya. As expatriates we felt free to wander into exotic Malindi Hotels like the Sinbad, enjoy the wonderful meals and endlessly long sandy beaches, and immerse ourselves in the coastal ambience. Doing anything together as a newly married couple was still a great joy, so to be exploring the exotic sights, sounds and smells of this tropical coastline was hugely enjoyable. So much so, that on the day of our departure we were reluctant to leave and delayed setting off back to Nairobi until the late afternoon.

It took about half an hour or so for the coconut palms to fade away and the sights, sounds and smells of the Coast to be replaced by the long gently climbing empty road leading into the hot inland plains. The car was going well and it was very exhilarating to be high speed cruising along the open road, windows wide open, watching the African sun make its plummeting descent into twilight time.

Shortly after Voi, about 120 miles from Mombasa, the road passes through Tsavo National Park. There were no fences separating Tsavo East from Tsavo West and in those days it was not uncommon to be charged by an angry rhino as you drove along. We happily zoomed along through the beautiful thorn tree bush. The light was just starting to fade. Trees grew close up to the edge of the road and long straight stretches were broken up with a few bends. We took one of these bends to find ourselves confronted immediately round the corner by a huge giraffe placed squarely on our side of the road and turned in towards the verge to browse off an overhanging acacia tree. Incidents with animals suddenly dashing into the road were common fare in our driving experience, but more usually in the form of a chicken or goat or cow or quite often a drunken man. Basically there were two options, slam on the brakes and crash at reduced speed into the obstruction or rapidly swerve around the animal or person. My reflexes were tuned into the rapid swerve around response option and without any touch on the brakes I immediately heeled over into the right hand lane to bi-pass the giraffe. To my horror, at the same instant the giraffe spun round into my lane, intending to bolt away to the other, probably clear, side of the road. The great beast was now squarely in front of us. There was no alternative but to hit the brakes. We slowed down a little from our 70 miles per hour cruising speed. A collision was inevitable and knowing how solid animals can be I thought this had to be the end. I managed to gasp out, "Sorry Miriam," and braced myself for the inevitable.

Amazingly, instead of smashing into one huge solid mass of flesh and bone there was a whoosh and a bit of a clunk and we were still moving down the Mombasa road intact. We instantly realised what must have happened. There was no way we could have missed that giraffe. Instead of crashing into the animal we had driven underneath its belly at what was probably about 60 miles per hour. Shaken, we pulled into the side of the road and looked back. There was no sign of the animal. We had definitely hit it a little bit and I imagined it was lying somewhere in the road injured. We drove back to look for it but could find no sign of the beast. Just as well. I'm not sure we could have done anything except put out branches to alert oncoming traffic. I tried to get out of the car but found the driver's door would not open. The passenger door was OK. Inspecting the car we found it was dented on the left side above my door. The PV was left-hand drive and we must have hit the hock of the giraffe's back leg as we went through. The windscreen was still intact and the roof was its normal shape. We must have just brushed the underbelly and glanced the top of a back leg. We hoped the giraffe also got off lightly. There was no sign of it. With the night now really starting to close in we switched on the headlights and continued much more slowly and on full alert all the way back to Nairobi. We were both stunned at what had happened. Had we really driven through the legs of a giraffe? We both concluded that amazing as it might seem that was the only possible reason why we were still in the land of the living.

When we finally got back to Nairobi, and the house of our good friends the Leach family, we regaled them with our account of our near miss. We even enacted what had happened on the living room floor. Although I know they would never doubt our integrity, I think they still found our story a bit hard to believe. In the morning when we went out to inspect the car in the daylight, besides the dent in the roof above my door there were thin strips of giraffe skin caught in both the left and the right rain guards. Conclusive proof of what had happened. They too were now thoroughly convinced. We really did drive through the legs of a giraffe at about 60 miles per hour on the Mombasa Road as it passes through Tsavo Game Park.

Immediately following this incident I used to tell the story to friends and visitors in Kenya. I think most of our close friends were convinced, but after leaving Kenya, the story did not carry. The impossibility of it was too much for them. People just did not believe me, so I became reluctant to talk about it. But watch a giraffe, particularly as it raises and extends its front legs to start loping off. There is lots of room under there, certainly enough for a PV Volvo.

Martin Horrocks, UK

The Hyena and the Film

The herd of elephants walked out of the acacia forest like gray ghosts. In spite of their great size they made no noise. The old matriarch of the herd led the way, closely followed by her babies. She stopped at the top of the riverbank and lifted her trunk to smell the wind. Sensing no danger, she cautiously slid down the steep bank and approached the small stream flowing through the golden sand. Her grown daughters and their babies followed in her footsteps and soon the entire matriarchal herd stood in a line with their trunks sucking up the cool clear water. They raised the tips of their water-filled trunks to their mouths and lifted their entire trunks, letting the water run into their throats.

Our camp stood on a bank of the Mwagusi sand river opposite the drinking elephants. I had come to the Ruaha National Park in southern Tanzania with my sons Jeff and Mike. We explored and took photographs in this largely unvisited wilderness - a location teeming with wildlife amidst a unique backdrop of granite boulders, palm trees, sand rivers and gigantic baobab trees.

After the elephants slaked their thirst, the adult females sucked up water in their trunks and blew the water on their backs and sides. The baby elephants lay down in the shallow water and rolled. Then they played king of the hill, climbing on top of each other under the watchful eyes of their mothers.

I had a sudden inspiration. Jeff was a senior at the Rift Valley Academy in Kenya and he needed a photograph of himself for the annual yearbook. I suggested he walk out on the sand river and pose in front of the elephants. Jeff didn't like the idea. I assured him elephants had bad eyesight and we were downwind from the elephants, so they were not aware of our presence. I convinced Jeff to stoop over and walk like a baboon, so the elephants would not notice him. Jeff finally agreed and hunched himself down and walked out on the open sand, carefully watching the elephants. The elephants paid no attention. When Jeff got within forty yards of the elephant herd, he slowly straightened up and faced the camera with a forced smile. I quickly took several photographs of him with the elephants in the background before Jeff dashed back to camp. He now had a great photograph for the yearbook.

I went to our Toyota Land Cruiser and took the roll of Kodak film out of the camera and put in a new one. Later we took down our tents, packed up our camp kitchen and headed back to Iringa town. When we got back to Iringa, I could not find the roll of film. Jeff felt he had risked his life for the photograph and now I'd lost the film.

Several months later two professional artists, Robb Glen and Sue Stolberger, visited the Ruaha National Park. They set up camp near the Mwagusi sand river. One afternoon Robb encountered a pride of lions laying on the track. He stopped his vehicle and watched as they slept and played. Suddenly a spotted hyena stepped out of the long grass. Lions and hyenas do not like each other since they both compete for the same prey. A large pack of hyenas will drive lions off their kill and steal the meat, but a lone hyena has no chance against a pride of lions. However, this hyena headed right toward the pride of lions. The lions crouched and waited. When the hyena got close, a lioness leaped up and smacked the hyena with its large paw, sending the hyena sprawling in the dust. Robb expected the wounded hyena to run away howling. Instead the hyena picked itself up and charged the lioness. The lioness attacked the hyena - using its claws and teeth. The hyena went down badly wounded, but it struggled to its feet and again attacked the lioness. The lioness finished off the hyena with a strangulating throat hold. Robb drove carefully around the lions and back to camp. He told Sue what he had seen and they tried to understand the hyena's odd actions.

The next day Robb drove down the same track. The lions had gone, but the hyena carcass had already started to rot and stink in the hot sun. The following day Sue drove down the same track and saw the rotting remains of the hyena, now mostly a mound of dark hair. Sue glimpsed something yellow. She stopped the vehicle and poked at the hyena carcass with a stick. Inside the stinking mess she found a dirty, dented roll of Kodak film. Gingerly she picked it up and placed it in a plastic bag.

Later she handed the film to Geoff Fox who owned one of the lodges in the park. He took it to Dar es Salaam and found a photo shop willing to process the film. Amazingly the film was still good and Geoff received a set of color prints with photos of a blond-haired boy standing in front of a herd of elephants. There was also a photograph of a white Toyota with the numbers of the license plate easily legible. When Geoff returned to the Ruaha National Park, he looked through the logbook at the entry gate. He matched the license plate number with my name and gave the photographs to his son Chris, who was a friend of mine.

Chris came to my camp near Iringa and jokingly accused me of dropping litter in the Ruaha Game Park. This confused me since I hadn't left anything in the park. Chris pulled out the photographs. When I saw the images of Jeff standing in front of a herd of elephants, I knew I had dropped the undeveloped roll of film in the park. When Chris told me the story of finding the film in the hyena, I did not really believe him. But over the next months I talked to each of the players separately and finally believed Sue had found my film in the stomach of a hyena.

I didn't tell my son. In July I spoke at the Commencement service for Jeff's graduation. I talked about the privilege of growing up in Africa and emphasized the unique things that can only happen in Africa. I told the story of Jeff posing in front of the elephants and my losing the film. Then I told the audience about finding the film inside the hyena. At the end of my talk I handed Jeff his senior photographs - a little late but uniquely developed in the stomach of a hyena.

Taken from Jon Arensen's memoir, Drinking the Wind

When Cultures Clash

The Naked District Officer

Noel Kennaway, a new District Officer (DO) posted to Turkanaland, set out on his first foot safari through his parish in early 1932. He wore a properly starched uniform as befitted a representative of the Crown. With the temperature above 100 degrees Fahrenheit and sweating profusely he quickly suffered from a severe case of chafing in some delicate parts of his anatomy. When his Turkana companions learned of his problem, they laughed and advised him to go around with no clothes on, just as they did. For the next four weeks, Kennaway traveled around naked, except for his sandals and official topi helmet. Returning to base he told his District Commissioner, Roland Baker-Beall, how he had solved his chafing problem.

Baker-Beall responded gravely. "Well, I'm not at all sure what you did was in order. I mean, we can't have His Majesty's officers walking around the district naked under nothing more than a helmet. Even if it doesn't affront the natives, what about the missionaries, eh? What about the missionaries?"

*From Ian Parker's book **Jua Kali's Voyage on the Jade Sea***

Milk for Sale

At Mariakani on the railway line, Africans would bring their produce to the train to sell it to the passengers. They brought oranges, mangoes, coconuts, and bottles of milk. The milk was extremely popular with South African troops in 1916 traveling up-country to fight with the British in the First World War. They bought so much milk that demand outstripped supply. A milk seller called for nursing mothers in the district to come and refill the milk bottles in a go-down at the Mariakani station. When authorities discovered this enterprising activity, there was a dramatic drop in the demand for milk along the entire length of the Uganda Railway.

*From Jennifer Stutchbury's unpublished manuscript, **Time's Eye***

Tea for Breakfast

About 1910 my father W J Dawson, known always as W J, bought the Plains Dairy, that vast flatland where the Nairobi Airport is today. He and three other young Scotsmen had great times in the corrugated iron house he built there. The others were George Taylor, Will Jaffray and Sandy Milne. One morning my father, who was always particular about his early morning tea, spat out the first mouthful in disgust at the taste. He went outside and asked George Taylor if he thought the tea undrinkable. Taylor replied, "I hadna' noticed." Father called the servant and asked where he had obtained the water for the tea. Imagine my father's reaction when the servant pointed to the tin bath in which all four men had bathed the evening before!

Belle Barker, Hermanus, South Africa

Cook Rescues Dahlias

My mother had a very spectacular garden on our farm during the 1940s. One year she decided to exhibit dahlias in the annual upcountry flower show. She grew particularly fine dahlias in every size, colour and hue. A few days before the long awaited flower show, the sky darkened and we heard a dreaded sound, like the cracking of bullets on the farmhouse tin roof - HAIL! My mother gave a fearful scream, "The dahlias!"

Everyone grabbed anything we could lay hands on - towels, tablecloths, even bedspreads, and we raced into the garden to cover the precious blooms from the terrible destruction of the hailstones. Our normally rather staid and dignified cook, not to be outdone, erupted from behind the house with a pile of washing off the line. I can see him tossing a pair of my father's khaki trousers over one of the prize blooms. His efforts helped my mother's dahlias survive to be exhibited in all their glory.

Margery Barnes, Naivasha

Why Fort Machakos was Attacked

J A Hunter once met an old Kamba man who had participated in an attack on the fort at Machakos many years before and almost wiped out the garrison. "Bwana," the old man said, "we weren't really interested in killing the soldiers. All we wanted was to get their empty cartridge cases. We used them for making snuff containers."

From African Bush Adventures by J A Hunter and Dan Mannix

Shukas Smell Bad

In the 1920s missionaries from Tenwek and Litein brought *shukas* to our village. We wondered at their white skin. They weren't black like us. They talked like birds and we couldn't understand them We children only wore animal skins for clothing. The missionaries encouraged us to wear the cloths. We accepted the gift, but once the missionaries left, we threw the *shukas* away. The cloth *shukas* smelled bad to our noses. We were also scared the white missionaries would eat us. Even when African evangelists came and called people to listen to God's Word, we children avoided them, thinking they'd come to eat us.

Sigila arap Cheptale, Maai Mahiu

Dried Locusts and Funerals

I am a Luyia from Bungoma and my late father, Henry Njite, told me the following stories about life in Kenya many years ago. While he was a boarder at Kima Boys Intermediate School in the 1930s they would often eat *ugali* with salt or dried locusts! Africans in those days who worked for Europeans often wondered how their employers knew certain things. For instance, a house worker would be sent to the butcher to buy meat, say ten pounds. On the way home the worker would cut off a pound to keep for himself. When he took the meat to the European's house, they discovered a piece of meat was not there! How did they know? Back in the kitchen there would be a scale to weigh the meat, which revealed a pound of meat had been taken. His employer would cut the man's salary to pay for the meat. Similarly, a man working in the garden (called a *shamba* 'boy' in those days) might be involved in some mischief, or he might rest from his work. He didn't know he was being watched from inside because the curtains on the window were not drawn. Many Africans used to think the spectacles Europeans wore helped them to see things others could not see.

An African worker would ask for permission to go home to attend the funeral of his father. After a while, the same man would go to his European employer and ask again to attend the funeral of his father. The European would wonder how many fathers this man had! The man would say the first one was his 'real' father because he was the cousin to his biological father. But this time, it really was his true biological father who had died. In the Luyia community, age-mates of one's father are also referred to as father, so the Luyia truly had many fathers. This was confusing for the Europeans to understand.

Hannington Henry Masiele, Maragoli

The Governor's Silver

My Grandfather Jock Harries, nick-named 'Black Harries,' arrived in Kenya in 1904. He was seconded from the Welsh Guards to the 4th King's Africa Rifles (KAR) in Uganda. In 1908, much to the annoyance of his parents, he gave up his army career and bought land at Njoro. However 1914 saw him back in the 4th KAR and with his battalion served between Voi and Mackinnon Road guarding the railway line against raiding Germans. Once the Germans had retreated across the border back to Tanganyika, the 4th KAR returned to Uganda, supposedly to protect the sources of the Nile and the lake steamer service. Back in Uganda he combined his military duties with hunting forays and the collecting of ivory all the way up to Jubaland. On one such safari he found himself camped next door to the Governor, who asked him over to dinner. He gladly accepted and attended with his batman in tow. The dinner went well and they exchanged many stories. The following morning he broke camp and was again on the march when a runner from the Governor's camp suddenly caught up with his safari, demanding the return of the silver. Shocked at the demand and accusation, Jock called up his batman to enquire what this was all about. "Well Sir," replied the batman, "I thought the Governor's tableware was a great improvement on ours and that the matter ought to be rectified." The silverware was returned.

Mike Prettejohn, Mweiga, Kenya

Meatball Assembly Line

My Mother arrived in Kenya in 1927 with us two boys aged three and four to join up with Dad who had gone on ahead to organise a house on a large tract of uninhabited bush-land between Eldoret and Kitale. Having a gathering of friends for even the simplest of occasions was never straightforward. One time, Mother instructed her kitchen staff to prepare a few snacks to go with the traditional sundowner routine. The food seemed to be delayed, so Mother went to the kitchen to investigate and hopefully to speed up the long awaited 'eats' – which consisted of meatballs made from a combination of mincemeat and mashed potato.

An inexplicable pause followed, interspersed with indistinguishable verbal outbursts. Finally Mother appeared with well-restrained apologies, leading a pair of well-groomed staff carrying trays of snacks.

The unexplained interval in the kitchen was soon forgotten

as the famished gathering began to eat and drifted into their familiar habit of storytelling. By the time a degree of satisfied digestion had taken place, Mother had a story of her own to tell about the delayed snacks.

Mother's surprise entry to the kitchen had disturbed a very successful operation by the cooks in producing the shapely meatballs. The fact that their speedy production line had been so comfortably rolled out from under their armpits seemed a completely unnecessary cause for the Memsahib's loud and astonished complaints!

Roy Marsh, Seychelles

Language Barrier

The North American nurse in the mission hospital struggled with her Swahili lessons. One day on the ward, she used her best Swahili to instruct one of the orderlies to perform some task. The orderly wasn't sure exactly what she wanted or whether she was even addressing him. So he put his finger to his own chest and questioned, "Mimi?" The frustrated nurse turned to him and said, "Yes, You You!"

Old Africa Editor

What Happened to Her Hair?

My wife, Daphne, was Private Secretary to Kenya's Governor, Malcolm MacDonald, and after independence to President Jomo Kenyatta. She was never happy with her hair and one day decided to have a 'perm.' When she returned from the hairdresser, an agitated office messenger asked one of my wife's colleagues whether Mrs Corner had become so poor that she could no longer have her hair straightened!

Dick Corner, South Africa

Muko Lak, Removing Teeth

I grew up at Ogada, a mission station in Luo country in western Kenya. On a lazy, warm afternoon a Luo friend and I were exploring about overgrown areas hunting birds with our slingshots, 'rahbahs' we called them. The name was derived from the English word rubber. We'd spent a couple of hours sneaking about in careful stalks of mouse birds, doves, guinea fowl and the like and were currently perched on a large rock overlooking a span of bush watching the bird activity. We must have been about seven or eight years old and the year was about 1943.

A couple of Luo men approached and said they had some business with my friend. He immediately became apprehensive and started to leave but was grasped firmly by the arm and held in place. The men explained that he was Luo and needed to join the tribe properly. It was time to remove his six lower permanent front teeth. My friend began to whimper and I objected saying they should let him go. The men said this was necessary and set him on the ground between one of the men's legs and knees where he was tightly squeezed by the man's arms. The second man took a short bladed knife from his pocket, forced my friend's mouth open and began to pry the front teeth, wedging the blade between them and slowly rotating it against adjacent teeth and levering upward to loosen their roots from the gum and bone.

I was not about to abandon my buddy but had no idea what I should do except stand by for him. With tears streaming down his face, he only occasionally cried out. When the teeth were loose, the man performing the surgery again pulled out a pair of pliers, which he used for the final removal. He then gave my friend a wad of green leaves tied into a small packet and told him to hold it tightly on the wound by biting down hard. They then released the lad, ruffled the top of his head, congratulated him on becoming a proper Luo and went on their way. The Luo call the rite *muko lak*, the removing of teeth.

Paul Skoda, Oregon, USA

Edible Cigarettes in Turkana

Back in 1958, Bob Simpson, Chris Eames and I loaded the dory and packed the car for a fishing trip to Lake Rudolf. We camped in Ferguson's Gulf on the west side of the lake. One day we decided to find the fresh-water Eliye Springs, which we had heard about. On landing the dory on the shore, some Turkana men appeared. They showed us the way to the springs, which were only about 100 metres from the lake's edge. When we were ready to leave they refused our thank you money, but happily accepted the few cigarettes I gave them. They ate them! We took a few minutes to show them how to light up and how to smoke and they smiled and laughed and when I gave them the rest of the pack, they proceeded to take the cigarettes out one by one, hand them solemnly around and once again they ate them!

Told by George Manuel and written by his daughter Hollie Manuel, Nakuru, Kenya

Don't Worry Memsaab!

We rented a house from an older settler lady in Mombasa. One day she told me how some years before her servant had walked right into her bedroom without knocking or saying, "Hodi!" She told him he shouldn't just walk into her bedroom with no warning. What if she had been getting dressed? "Don't worry, Memsaab," was the man's reply. "I always look in through the window first before opening the door to your bedroom."

Bud MacDougall, Canada

Kuja Hapa

Hoppy Marshall, the Hangman in Kenya in the 1940s, had made several attempts at the Standard Swahili Exam. At his final exam he confidently answered the preliminary questions correctly. Then the examiner said to him, "Tell me to come to you."

"*Kuja hapa*," Hoppy replied happily.

"Now tell me to go over there to that corner of the room," the examiner instructed.

Hoppy thought for a moment, then strode over to the place indicated and said, "*Kuja hapa.*"

I believe he passed the exam!

Nancy Fairclough, formerly of Kilifi and Kabete

Coffee Filter

I was holding one of my regular dinner parties at my farmhouse near Tigoni in the 1930s. All went well and afterwards coffee was served. My guests thought the coffee to be excellent and asked how it had been made. I had no idea, so I called my cook and asked him in front of my guests how he managed to obtain such a delicate flavour. "I strained it through one of your socks, Bwana," was the reply. Then seeing the look of horror on the faces of the assembled company he quickly added, "Oh, but it wasn't a *clean* sock Bwana…!"

by John Downey, as told by Margaret Downey, Langata

Shady Aeroplane

Martin and Osa Johnson used to fly around East Africa in an aeroplane painted with zebra stripes. When they landed on the edge of Lake Rudolph a number of Turkana came by to see the plane. Johnson asked one of the Turkana what he thought of the plane. The man nodded and answered: "It gives a nice shade for sitting under."

Robert Matthews, Kent

Beehive Deception

A young Dorobo man wanted a wife. To woo the young lady named Naipuyupui, he exaggerated about his wealth, telling her he had many beehives in the forest. In reality, he only had one. After making the marriage arrangements, the man took his bride home. After sleeping one night, Naipuyupui asked to see his beehives. He led her into the forest and showed her his beehive. "My first beehive is this one," he said. Happy to have married such a rich Dorobo man, Naipuyupui asked to see the other hives. The man led her by a circuitous route through the forest and came back to the same beehive from behind. "This is my second hive," he said. They went back into the forest and this time approached the same beehive from another angle. "This is my third beehive," the man lied. He pushed on, then knelt behind a bush from where it was barely possible to catch of glimpse of the same hive. "There's another," he said. They walked a long time and from another ridge he pointed across the trees to where you could just make out the lid of the beehive. "That one's mine as well," he said.

They went home, Naipuyupui pleased that her husband would provide her with lots of honey. After the rains when the trees had flowered, Naipuyupui asked her husband to harvest some honey. He went into the forest and came back with his leather honey bag full of honey. Soon Naipuyupui wanted more.

"The hive is empty," her husband said.

"Go to one of your other hives," she said.

"They are too far way," he answered.

"What do you mean, too far away?" she asked. "You showed me all your hives in one day."

The man had to admit he had tricked her. Naipuyupui forced him to make more hives by telling her neighbours to help her husband because he only had one beehive.

told by Daniel ole Kashu of Narianta, Kenya, who heard the story from his grandmother.

Bad Binoculars

As we drove up the Subukia road towards Lake Hannington (now Lake Bogoria) in 1965, my husband Victor Burke stopped to watch some birds with his binoculars. Within minutes six Tugen men had gathered, intrigued by the binoculars. Victor explained that the binoculars brought things closer. Victor handed the binoculars to the men to try. They took turns looking through the binoculars, turning them this way and that. Finally they handed the binoculars back and told Victor they were no good. "You told us they would bring things closer so we could see them," one man said, "but we can't see the wedding that we know is taking place on the other side of that mountain!"

From Margaret Ann Hayes' book **Safarini**

Arrested for Not Working

My late father, Henry Njite, was the son of David Ogonda Njite who converted to Christianity very early and went to school. My grandfather belonged to the Church of God and went on to become a schoolteacher. He, therefore, took my father to school at Kima, the headquarters of the Church of God. After school, my father was taken for further training in agriculture. After this training the colonial government, who had spent money for his agricultural training, expected him to work for them. My father refused and went to Kitale where he founded a music band. The government arrested my father and gave him an ultimatum after some days in custody. He could stay in prison or agree to be employed with the agricultural department. My father chose the latter and worked at many stations (Nakuru, Molo, Thomson's Falls, Kaimosi, Kitale, Njoro, Vihiga and finally Kakamega) before retiring in the 1970s.

Hannington Henry Masiele, Maragoli, Kenya

Spaghetti Machine

One bright, sunny, Sunday afternoon at Rift Valley Academy (RVA), Kijabe, during the 1940s the English worship service had just concluded and the participants were visiting on the front veranda. As a teen-aged RVA student, I walked with some of my schoolmates back to the student lounge through the crowd of missionaries and some nearby settler farmers.

I overheard the wife of a settler who had a ranch at the base of the escarpment telling an interesting anecdote. The rancher had bought a new 10-ton hydraulic jack, which he used on the farm. A few days earlier the jack disappeared. He searched but could not find it anywhere on the premises. There ensued *barazas* with farm workers and the typical exclamations, "We have not seen it, Bwana...!" The exasperated rancher threatened all sorts of penalties, fines, even police action – all without results!

On the ranch there was a camp of Italian POWs building the escarpment road, as well as a small Catholic chapel. Following up on a tip offered by some nameless person, the rancher visited the kitchen in the POW camp. He finally spotted his 10-ton jack, neatly installed in a jerry-rigged machine for extruding pasta – spaghetti or macaroni!

Richard Adkins, USA

The Swahili Exam

In the Kenya Police in the late 1940s, in order to progress up the salary scale one had to qualify in various ways, including having the ability to speak and write good Swahili. The regular examinations were a nightmare for most of us, especially if conducted by Sir Howard Elphinstone, an enthusiastic adherent of the classic Oxford references **Standard Swahili-English Dictionary** and its counterpart **Standard English-Swahili Dictionary**.

Generally one could get by with so-called 'Kitchen Swahili.' As an example, I shall always remember hearing the following order barked out at a top class hotel in Nairobi: "Kwenda upstairsie, lookie behind doorie and lete coatie hanging uku!"

Back to the Police Swahili exams, I knew a well-respected elderly officer, whom I shall call Tom, whose progress had been stymied by this confounded Kiswahili Examination. The oral part of the exam comprised a short interview with Sir Howard and his Mswahili assistant Juma. They started with customary salutations and progressed to a more challenging examination, even to some translation of the law.

The dreaded day arrived and Tom, well known to Sir Howard, put in his usual appearance. After Tom managed the greetings, Sir Howard, who undoubtedly had a soft spot for the old 'battler' asked, smiling: "Tom, how would you say 'A froggy would a wooing go?'"

Tom froze. Rising from his chair he said, "Thank you Sir Howard. I'll see you next year."

Feeling sorry for Tom, Sir Howard said, "Listen, I am going to hand over to our old friend Juma and let him suggest something which you might translate into English."

Juma offered Tom the phrase: "Haraka haraka, haina baraka." (Hurry hurry is without blessing.)

After a moment's hesitation, Tom tried, "Hark, hark, the dogs do bark?"

Brian Boulton, Western Australia

It's Not a Cow!

One day I decided to have a little fun with a Maasai man near Kajiado where I worked at the AIC Child Care Centre. I had a photograph of a longhaired Scottish cow and I showed it to this man. "*Enkiteng ena,*" I said using my best Maasai to say this is a cow. The Maasai man shook his head and said it wasn't a cow. Thinking he didn't recognise the "cowness" of the animal under the shaggy hair, I insisted it was a cow. He kept saying it wasn't. Finally I said, "It's still a cow even if it has long hair. It's how cows look in Scotland. Why won't you believe me?" The Maasai man smiled and said adamantly, "It's not a cow. *Olkiteng ele*. It's a bull!"

Georgie Orme, Scotland

Mrs Pagoda and the Bamboo Shoots

In late 1959 I worked as a Forester at Fort Essex, which became Kimakia Forest Station, on the southern Aberdare Mountains about 35 miles up from Thika. The resident labour of this forest station had over four acres of land to cultivate on the '*Shamba*' system of converting grassland (bamboo) to, mainly, soft wood plantations. In addition the Forest and Agricultural Departments encouraged them to keep grade sheep. As an extra bonus in this area, these workers were cutting leading shoots from the new bamboo culms that grow at a very fast rate, and are branchless until reaching full height. Kenya Canners in Thika purchased these shoots, provided they were not over about eighteen inches long, nor over about one-and-a-half inches in diameter. Trucks from Kenya Canners would collect them from the Forest Station – roads and weather permitting – and they paid the labourers cash for bundles of about twelve bamboo shoots. Back in Thika, they treated the shoots and canned them under the label of "Three Cooks."

The bamboo shoots proved to be very popular with the general public, so the powers-that-be at Kenya Canners organised a Field Day at the Forest Station for members of their staff, Forest, Agricultural and Administrative Staff and other invited people. The most important guest was 'Mrs

Pagoda' – actually Cheri Black, the proprietor of the Pagoda Restaurant, I think the first and only Chinese Restaurant in Nairobi at that time. The great day came and we watched the harvesting, preparation, purchase and removal of this wonderful commodity. After refreshment there was general talk and congratulations. At this stage someone asked Mrs Black what she thought of the bamboo shoots and their preparation. Her reply went roughly like this – "I do not think there is a word for it in Chinese – but I think in English it is *rubbish*." Now here was a dampener! Not long after this the trucks from Kenya Canners in Thika ceased to come up to the Forest Station and "Three Cooks Bamboo Shoots" were no longer found on the shelves of our grocery stores!

Andrew Challoner, Gilgil

USAID Unappreciaided

In the mid-1960s I was the district veterinary officer in Lango, a district in central Uganda bounded on the west by the Nile and on the east by Karamoja district. The district headquarters was the town of Lira on the main road from Mbale to Gulu in the northern district of Acholi. Milk in Lira was sold on an informal basis with milk producers pedalling around the houses of regular customers on their bicycles with milk in a churn fixed to their carriers and ladling out whatever amount was required which prudent consumers would then boil. What was not sold was unloaded on the Lira Dairy Cooperative, a small block-built structure with a galvanized iron roof, in the town centre for sale there. There was, however, a downside to this latter arrangement as the cooperative charged a cess, which found little favour with the producers. This was no surprise for previously when I had been working in the Kabaka's government in Buganda I had found that dairy farmers much preferred marketing their own milk, even though it took up three to four hours of their time each day, in preference to selling it to a dairy.

The Cold War was at its hottest in the mid-1960s and the two major powers were competing for alliances with the newly independent African countries. In a fit of unthinking charity the United States Agency for International Development (USAID) donated a milk-cooling machine to the Lira Dairy Cooperative and in due course a beautiful stainless steel cooler was delivered to the cooperative's premises. The back wall of the dairy was knocked down so it could be installed and it was duly set up and the wall rebuilt. But it didn't work because, being American, it operated at 110 volts and the local supply sometimes approximated 240 volts. The back wall was knocked down again and the cooler sent away for alterations before being returned and the wall bricked up yet again. Meanwhile the Town Council, under pressure from central authorities, passed a by-law prohibiting the informal sale of milk in the township.

This did not go down well with the producers who got a lower price for their milk. It also did not go down well with the district medical officer who realised bulking up the milk supplies in the cooler in the absence of a pasteurizing unit meant any contaminant (tuberculosis and salmonellosis were his main concerns) would now be distributed to all milk consumers in the town and not just to a section of consumers.

But the final irony was that the cooler was turned off every night to allow the milk to sour before the morning because the Langi preferred their milk that way — a preference many African people show and may well be related to the high rate of lactose intolerance in some African populations.

*From Roland Minor's book, **A Lot of Loose Ends***

They Call the Wind Mariyah

My wife Diane and I lived in Idi Amin's Uganda for two years in the early 1970s, where I taught Sociology at Makerere University, and she taught music at Kitante Primary School. While there, Diane played the piano and I sang whenever we had the opportunity.

One night we participated in a musical variety program at the Uganda National Theatre. The show included Indian sitar music and dancing, Baganda drums and amadinda (xylophone), and European music, both instrumental and vocal. Accompanied by Diane, I began to belt out my first number "They Call the Wind Mariyah." A ripple of laughter passed through the primarily Baganda audience. As I sang, the laughter increased, and Diane became increasingly upset. I thought to myself: "Aha, they haven't heard a trained European-type voice," and I bellowed louder. By the time I reached the last line, they were rolling in the aisles. Pulling ourselves together, Diane and I went on to our second selection, and politeness reigned, followed by enthusiastic applause.

At the intermission, I made my way back to the theatre lobby, where they served sodas and snacks. While waiting to order, I noticed a small, white-haired lady had slipped up beside me. "Mr. Adams," she asked quietly, "would you like to know why they were laughing?"

"Yes, I certainly would."

"Well, you know, in the Luganda language 'l' and 'r' are the same letter."

"So to their ears what was I singing?"

"Maliya," she stated gently, "is the Luganda word for prostitute."

No wonder the audience laughed at lines like: "Before I knew Mariyah's name, and heard her wail and whining," and especially the last line: "Blow my love to me."

I was unable to sing that song for at least ten years without laughing. And the experience taught Diane and me how important it is, if you are going to live in someone else's society, to know something of the language and culture of the people among whom you are a visitor.

Bert N. Adams, Professor Emeritus of Sociology,
University of Wisconsin

Where is Kite Tail?

Some American tourists stopped me and asked if I knew the way to Kite Tail.

"Where?" I asked, puzzled.

"Kite Tail," they repeated. "We are driving to Kite Tail, and we're not sure we're on the right road."

I shook my head. "No, I don't know of any place called Kite Tail."

"Aren't you from Kenya?" they asked. "We hear Kite Tail is a big town and you say you've never heard of it?"

"Maybe if you spell it for me," I replied, wondering if their American accent prevented me from understanding them.

"Kite Tail is spelled K-I-T-A-L-E," they said. Mystery solved.

Shirley Poole, Naivasha

Feeding the troops in Burma

My parents, Dr Igor and Erica Mann, came to Africa as refugees in the Second World War. They travelled by foot from Romania to Israel and were in a queue to board a ship to take them to the United States. As they approached the officer who was taking people's names and assigning 'tickets,' another officer came up to talk to him and my mother (who knew sufficient English) distinctly heard the word 'veterinarian.' My father had been a well-known veterinarian in Europe, so when my mother came up to the officer at the desk she said, "My husband veterinarian." They were promptly removed from the line and assigned to travel to Rhodesia, where they needed a vet to organise the cattle. My mother said she was thrilled, as she had always wanted to go to Africa.

They stayed in Rhodesia for a while, but the work with cattle never really happened as there just weren't any! They shipped my father up to Kenya to look after Liebig's Meat Factory that became The Kenya Meat Commission in Athi River.

One of the main functions of the factory at the time was to produce cans of corned beef for the troops in North Africa and Burma. My mother helped my father in the laboratory of the factory. She was an architect and very artistically-inspired, so she designed the label for the corned beef going to Burma. The label portrayed the upper half of a smiling strong man flexing his bulging arm muscles. It was a visually beautiful label and everyone was very proud of the first big shipment.

A few weeks later – as long as freight and messages took to travel in those days – everyone was shocked and astounded to hear there had been a near-mutiny amongst the African troops in Burma when the beautifully labeled cans of meat arrived. It took a while to find out what the trouble was. It turned out they thought a can with a label picturing a strong man must mean the can contained human meat! No one would eat it and they preferred to starve if that was necessary.

Learning the shocking news, my mother quickly made another, plainer and more acceptable, label. An airplane carried a special shipment of the new labels to Burma. The cans were re-labelled, the soldiers were fed, happy and fought well, and all came to a happy conclusion.

Oscar Mann, Nairobi

Rolling Stone

While stationed in Nairobi in the late 1950s, my wife and I, and our young son Charles spent our holidays at Amboseli. There were seasons when the National Park was closed because of temporary flooding of the drifts in the low-lying country. Often the roads were impassable to non-4WD vehicles and we did not have 4WD so we usually avoided the area in the wet season. However, on one occasion when we were in the park, an unexpected storm and consequent flash floods entailed seeking help. The park warden, 'Tabs' Taberer, suggested he escort us from Ol Tukai Lodge to 'Budge' Gethin's Hotel at Namanga. Setting out early, we splashed our way to a drift just a couple of miles short of Namanga, only to find that it was in spectacular spate. Nothing daunted, Tabs had his rangers make a fire and soon had the kettle boiling while we settled down in our camp chairs to wait.

Eventually, Tabs called over a ranger and told him to place a stone at the water's edge so he could judge whether the spate was receding. We settled down to more mugs of tea and much chatter. One of the rangers had become a particular *rafiki* of our son, so it was not long before Charles was shrieking with delight as the ranger raced him around in his push-chair, often down to the water's edge.

After a couple of hours and with more storm clouds gathering, Tabs went to inspect the water's edge, where the stone still marked the water line. As we watched him standing there, he called over the ranger and had a heated discussion. Coming back to us, Tabs told us to pack up our car and follow him across the drift, which had receded enough for us to cross.

Apparently, the ranger had assumed the stone was to be kept at the water's edge so, as the water had gone down, he had moved the stone accordingly!

Brian Boulton, Australia

Eviction Notice from a Baobab Tree

During the building of the Makupa causeway, over the shallow section of sea separating the west of Mombasa island from the mainland, some baobabs that were in the way had to be felled. One very old and revered tree was destined for destruction. For centuries this tree had been regarded as the home of the devil – shaitani – and the workmen refused to touch it. The nonplussed government engineer hit on an imaginative idea. He nailed upon the baobab a notice to quit, ordering the evil spirit to find another abode within seven days. After the prescribed week the workmen were quite happy to fell the tree, because the spirit had been given due warning.

From C S Nicholls's memoir, ***A Kenya Childhood***

Ribbon-Man

Every town has its memorable street-characters…Geita has Mlozi. He's between twenty and thirty, people think. According to his late mother, he was born in the year of the 'great rain.' This pins it down nicely. The monsoons bring big rains *every* year… Mlozi's age is approximate.

He sits on a huge *mwamba* or flat granite rock at the end of Top Road…He's there every day, from sunrise till after sunset. He sleeps somewhere on the compound, although nobody knows were. Somebody's sheltering and feeding him, because Mlozi does nothing except sit and talk to himself, yet, though filthy and odoriferous, he looks in good health.

He wears strips of cloth…purposefully torn ribbons of fabric, of every colour. Where he gets it, nobody knows. He wears a *moochi* made of strips of green, red, orange and blue cloth, all knotted together, only just preserving his modesty. Sometimes. There are torn coloured ribbons plaited into his thick, overgrown hair and wispy beard. More round his forehead and neck. He is truly Ribbon-Man.

He has *mifupa*, or bones. At least a dozen are tied round each ankle on thin rawhide cords. They're dry, make a rattling sound when he moves. Lutoli says they're chicken bones, so they don't really count in *ishara*, or omen, terms…

He talks to himself constantly. A whispering commentary, which sounds like two different voices, one male, the other female, giving different views about mundane things. I find it strange, because everyone can *see* the sun's up, the birds are in the sky, *watu* are walking past and the hills are all around. Say something I *don't* know, I think, as Lutoli and I stand and listen. Sometimes he reads my thoughts, leaps to his feet, violently shakes his Kimbo-tin full of stones, producing a very loud rattle, and shouts. "*Kwenda wewe!*"…His eyes bulge like a frog's, veins stand out on his neck. The Kimbo-rattle alone is enough to send Lutoli and I running. Yet we find Ribbon-Man irresistibly magnetic. It becomes a game of dare. How long dare we stay before we run? Dread, fear, delicious panic. Beats boredom.

As time passes, we flee less quickly…

From James Penhaligon's memoir, **Speak Swahili Dammit!**

School Stories

Moostaken Identity

As a schoolboy at Duke of York School in the 1950s, I remember a group of soldiers from the Black Watch who guarded the school. They built a tower by the edge of the school and armed soldiers kept watch from their perch for any Mau Mau intruders. One night we heard three blasts from their rifles. We grabbed our hockey sticks and ran to the windows, ready to defend our school. Nothing happened. We waited. Everything stayed calm. In the morning we went out to find what the soldiers had been firing at. Three dead cows, belonging to the headmaster, lay near the guard tower, gunned down in the night as suspected Mau Mau attackers.

Tony Monkhouse, Naivasha

Rugby Pitch Explodes

When I was a student at Prince of Wales School during the Abysinnian Campaign of World War II, the school was evacuated from Nairobi to the old Sparks Hotel in Naivasha (now Naivasha Country Club). We wanted a place to play rugby so we cleared a rugby pitch below the hotel down by the lake's edge. We slashed down bushes, cut down papyrus, and raked all the cuttings into piles. We set fire to the mounds of rubbish and stood back. Soon loud explosions ripped loose from underneath our bonfires of brush sending us running. Apparently old ammunition from years before had been dumped in the lake. As the lake level had dropped, these ammunition stores were now buried just inches below the grass and our fires set it off.

Geoff Irvine, Naivasha

Don't Shoot!

During the Mau Mau emergency the Inniskilling Fusiliers were posted to Duke of York School to guard us from possible attack as the school bordered the Kikuyu reserve. However, it proved a mixed blessing for the teaching staff. If any of them ventured abroad after dark, the Fusiliers took a fiendish delight in jumping out from behind bushes, pointing their .303 rifles in their directions and yelling at them to reveal their identities. This was the soldiers' way of relieving the tedium, I imagine, as the Honourable Charles Kitchener, younger son of Kitchener of Khartoum and my old Housemaster, could hardly have been mistaken for a Mau Mau. When challenged, the master would raise his hands and cry out, "Don't shoot!" We school boys, watching delightedly from our dormitory windows, would mutter, "Why not?"

Tony Massie-Blomfield, Nairobi

The Forgotten Violin

My sister Wanda Vincenzini and I climbed on board the E A R & H train in Nairobi in 1946 or 1947 for the trip upcountry to Eldoret where we were boarding students at the Eldoret Convent. As we loaded our bags onto the train, my sister realised she had forgotten her violin at home. Our mother said, "No worries," and she rushed back to where we lived at the time near Westlands. She collected my sister's violin and waited for the train to pass by one of the level crossings near the shops at Westlands. The engineer saw this lady standing at the level crossing waving him down with the violin in her hand. He slowed down and we leaned out of the window and grasped the forgotten violin! Further along the railway line we reached the Prince of Wales School. The boys knew we were on our way to Eldoret and as the train struggled slowly uphill they came down to the railway line and managed to jump on and off the train for quite a distance, much to the dismay of the nuns escorting us!

Liliana Ciardi, Spain

Wattle Underwear?

While attending the Highlands High School at Eldoret, we were taken to a wattle farm belonging to an elderly German. Wattle trees were grown and the bark used for the leather tanning industry. We were told how the trees were planted and harvested and finally to our great amusement he said, "Und von day you vill all be verring vattle underver. Ve vill turn the trees into fine thread like nylon." Thank goodness that never happened. Imagine wattle underwear! Would it have been scratchy and bright yellow, like the flowers?

We had lunch in the wattle plantation and then went for a dip in the small river. When we got out, we were horrified to find we were covered with leeches! We received no sympathy from our teachers who informed us that the Victorians paid doctors good money to bleed them with leeches.

Helen Leggatt, South Africa

Ivory Tower

In 1920 after several requests by the Government, a school for chief's sons and others was begun in Juba, Sudan – four Acholi boys being the first boarders. It is recorded that the first of these arrived with three porters and a tusk of ivory to pay his school fees!

from an unpublished paper written by Leonard Sharland, submitted by his son Dr Roger Sharland, Nairobi

Catching the Train

Getting out into the bush was the best thing about going to school at Rift Valley Academy for me. We had a huge playground – the wild out-of-doors. Once we hiked a few miles northwestward along the railway to climb Kijabe Hill. We found heavy old tires near the top and sent them crashing down the mountain, squashing bushes. We laughed hard when a reedbuck and a duiker ran for their lives. Coming back we ran and climbed on a freight train chugging uphill. Didgie (Dave Johnson) missed getting on with the rest of us, so he caught the caboose. Hanging on, he looked up – into the black-bearded brown face of an Indian Sikh with neat red turban.

"Yes, how far?" the Sikh man said in a deep friendly voice.

Stanley Barnett in an unpublished memoir

Water Coming!

I boarded as a pupil at Nairobi Girl's School in the early 1930s. I clearly remember our baths. The bathroom had wooden cubicles and cement floors with a 'ditch' at the back. Each cubicle had a wooden rack on the floor and a galvanized iron tub. We had to fill a pail with hot water from a tap outside the cubicles. When we finished our baths, we would stand on the wooden rack and shout, "Water coming!" and then tip the tub toward the 'ditch.' As the walls were about six inches above the floor, the water would flood into adjoining cubicles – hence the necessity of the rack and the warning shout!

Anne Robertson (nee Johanson), Hemmingford, Canada

Climbing Mount Longonot

Soon after the outbreak of World War 2 we boarders from the Prince of Wales School were moved to the old Sparks Hotel at Naivasha because the military required our school building at Kabete for a military hospital. We boys regarded our time at Naivasha like a long holiday, but they required us to work at our lessons as well. The spacious school grounds extended down to Crescent Island Lake. Sunday afternoons we could roam where we wished – only the *dukas* in Naivasha town were out of bounds.

One Sunday afternoon three of us decided to climb Mt

Longonot. As soon as lunch ended, we left the school grounds and crossed over the South Lake Road. We headed across a vast empty plain for Mt Longonot, miles away on the horizon. We set off at a fairly fast but sustainable run. There were no roads or tracks to follow but the grazing Tommies, Grants, and zebra had kept the grass down and the going was easy.

By mid afternoon we reached the base of Longonot. We looked up the bush-covered slope and decided to give it a go to the rim. We climbed up a steep ridge following a game track. We paused near the rim when we heard the crashing of bushes. Several buffalo galloped down past us on an adjacent ridge a few yards away from where we stood. Soon we stood on the rim of the crater and looked down its bush-covered walls. We didn't spend long there but turned our attention to the return journey. We couldn't see the school, but we made out its position by the glint of Crescent Island Lake.

We were soon off the mountain, but we still had a daunting distance to cover to get back in time for Sunday evening prayers. We kept running, helped by the cooling afternoon. Darkness fell as we reached the school. We just had time to put on ties and pull on long trousers and change into blazers before joining the other boys trooping into service.

John Poulton, Portugal

Cycling Home from School

David Forrester, Birro Aagaard and I decided to cycle home from the Prince of Wales School in December 1949. Birro was to spend part of the holiday with David at Rumuruti, and my parents had a farm near Ol Joro Orok. For some practice during the term we, and three others, cycled to Longonot Railway Station, leaving our bikes in the kindly care of the Indian stationmaster, climbed to the peak and then rode back to school.

The round trip was about 70 miles, to say nothing of the several thousand feet of altitude change.

We had planned to leave school at about 2 am but, as no one was checking us out, at 9 pm we decided to go in the lovely clear night. With loaded bikes it was a bit of a slog up to the edge of the Rift, followed by a glorious free-wheel down to the Italian Chapel. As we passed the Chapel a lorry drew alongside and the nice Indian driver offered us a lift to Naivasha, which we accepted with alacrity.

The ride from Naivasha to Gilgil along the flat went well and we turned off the tar onto the Ol Kalau road at about 4 am. The rough, stony road and the steep climb up past Pembroke College exhausted us, so at 5 am we decided to stop for an hour's kip in the ditch. Then we were off on a more level road to Ol Joro Orok, where we arrived soon after Mr Unia had opened his shop for business. He kindly let us have some biscuits and pop 'on tick', and I was able to phone home.

We rode on a couple of miles to our friends the Gaddums, who worked on the Agricultural Research Station. My mother collected us and took us to our farm for a good breakfast, rest and lunch. She then drove David and Birro back to the Gaddums, where they collected their bikes and rode on to Rumuruti, arriving safely before dark.

Richard Truran, Exeter, UK

The Lord's Business

Papa Skoda on the Lord's Business

Papa Skoda, a missionary working in Ogada, could really shake the piano when he played, but he didn't know much about car maintenance. I spent a high school vacation in the 1950s with the Skodas when my father was sick. Seeing the state of Papa Skoda's car, I carried my small toolkit with me one Sunday as we headed to church. Papa Skoda frowned at the toolbox in my hand. "We're on the Lord's business, Dilly. Leave your tools behind. God will take care of our car." Reluctantly, I put my toolbox back in the house.

As we slithered along the muddy roads, the car got stuck in a ditch. "Should I get out and push?" I offered.

"No need," Papa Skoda countered. "We're on the Lord's business. He'll get us out of the mud."

Papa Skoda climbed out of the car, stood in front of the mired vehicle and prayed. He got back in and the car eased its way out of the mud. Every time we got stuck, he refused my offer to push and reminded me we were on the Lord's business. After a prayer we always got out of the mud and the car, miraculously, managed to run all day. I learned a lot about faith the day I accompanied Papa Skoda on the Lord's business.

Dilly Andersen, Timau

Manna from Heaven?

Alfred Swann left his missionary post on Lake Tanganyika in 1886 for a rest in England. He chose to walk south towards Lake Nyasa intending to reach the coast via the Zambezi River. As he passed along the high plateau occupied by the Amambwi tribe, the people showed him a curious white substance on the ground early in the morning before the sun rose.

At first Swann wondered how porridge had been scattered on the ground. He knelt down to examine it more closely. The white substance looked like hoarfrost and resembled coriander seeds. Swann tasted some and described it as sweet. The Amambwi people told him it melted in the sun and if you kept it overnight it would be full of worms in the morning. But if they baked it, they could keep it for a while without spoiling. The Amambwi could only gather it with permission from the chief.

Swann asked them where it came from. The Amambwi answered: "It's the food of God! No one knows where it comes from."

Swann knew the biblical account of God feeding the Israelites with manna in Exodus 16. The manna appeared in the morning like frost. It melted in the sun. It was white like coriander seed and tasted like honey. If kept overnight, it crawled with maggots and stunk. Could this be the manna described in the Bible?

Swann set out to discover the source. He wondered if some insects unearthed it during the night, but could find no holes near the sweet white manna. Tiny fungi sprang up the next night on the spot where the manna melted, so he thought maybe the white stuff was mushroom spawn. But Swann could never identify the source of the manna.

Swann reported in his book that a few years later some other Europeans travelling in that area saw the same white manna. They baked a cake of it and sent it to England, but no one could determine its identity.

From Alfred J Swann's book,
Fighting the Slave Hunters in Central Africa

A Hole in his Trousers

Rev P A Bennett, an Anglican missionary in the early 1900s in Kenya, arrived to hold a church service at a settler's house one Sunday and discovered a hole in the seat of his trousers caused by rubbing back and forth on the wooden seat of his tonga as he bounced about on bush roads and rough tracks. On his stipend, Bennett couldn't afford another pair of trousers. But his host that day gave Bennett a pair of pants with holes in the knees. By wearing both pairs of trousers at the same time, Bennett covered both sets of holes and was able to carry out his church duties in respectable clothing.

*From H K Binks' book **African Rainbow***

Donkeys in Trousers and Jackets

Albert Cook, a missionary doctor, walked to Uganda in 1896 with 54 donkeys, some for carrying packs and white Muscat donkeys for riding. He decided to protect the donkeys from tsetse fly bites as they crossed the fly-infested plains lying inland from the Kenya coast. He didn't know at the time that the tsetse fly bites were almost always fatal to pack animals. He did know that when the flies bit the donkeys, they reared and bucked and ran helter-skelter, scattering their loads as they went. The resulting chaos could delay the caravan for hours, maybe days. So Cook provided his donkeys with trousers and jackets made from Amerikani cloth. Thanks to those trousers and jackets, which prevented tsetse fly bites, the donkeys survived the journey to Uganda.

From Jennifer Stutchbury's unpublished manuscript,
Time's Eye

Hitler in Heaven

During World War II a gifted Italian artist was incarcerated as a Prisoner of War in Kenya. A nearby mission asked if this artist could paint a mural in their church. On the request of the good fathers he was temporarily released from camp and started the work. The artist painted on the condition that no one should view the mural until completion.

On unveiling, a beautifully rendered scene depicted heaven above and hell below. On closer inspection, the fathers were rather shocked to find that two of the little cherubs floating above in heaven sported the faces of Hitler and Mussolini, and a couple of horned devils below bore the distinct features of Churchill and Roosevelt!

Elio Balletto, Malindi

Church Service Interrupted

A visiting minister came to a farmer's home in the 1950s to conduct the monthly church service. As the congregation settled into their seats in the living room, a hen, disturbed from her normal nesting place on an old sofa on the veranda, deposited her egg with an ear-splitting cackle and departed indignantly in a flurry of feathers. The pianist struck up the first hymn on the old piano stationed outside the window, prompting one of the farm dogs to howl in a mournful falsetto. The rest of the pack, disturbed by the sudden hullabaloo, decided this was a chance to settle old scores, and piled onto the howling dog and a king-sized dogfight erupted on the lawn.

The householder strode out of the house, called for a bucket of water, and with a decidedly unchristian oath, threw it over the protagonists. Peace was finally restored and the service continued without further incident.

Margery Barnes, Naivasha

Preacher Forgets Wedding

During the early years of Kenya's independence, I was privileged to work with the rapidly developing church in Uasin Gishu District, the area around Eldoret where I was stationed. As the only local ordained minister for our denomination at that time, my Saturdays were often spent conducting weddings. Some months ahead of time I had settled on a date to marry a couple in adjacent Keiyo District.

Somehow I forgot about that appointment. I thought I had a free Saturday so my wife and I went for a long walk that afternoon. When we arrived home pretty late I was shocked out of my leisurely stroll to find some church leaders on our doorstep enquiring whether I was still going to conduct the marriage! We hurried to the wedding venue in far away Metkei location of Keiyo (then known as El-Geiyo) arriving after dark much to the relief of the waiting couple and guests.

I was mortified when they apologised for having had the feast that afternoon before the marriage ceremony (which had been scheduled for the morning) – but they had kept food for me! My sincere apologies and *mutyo mising* (very sorry) were accepted with such grace. I would never slip up again in that manner!

Jack Pienaar, Cape Town

Close Call

During the Simba Rebellion in Congo in 1962-63 Dr Ray Williams worked as the surgeon at a mission hospital at Mulongo. When he was at the hospital early one morning, some soldiers came in shooting. Dr Williams waved a white flag. But bullets continued to fly. Dr Williams hid inside the X-ray room. When the sound of gunfire stopped, Dr Williams slipped out to see what was going on. He saw his house had been set on fire. Knowing he had a lot of books in the house – many of them borrowed – he ran to the house, pulled open the back door and started throwing books out the back windows. As the fire intensified, he ran out of the front door to escape the flames. He met a group of soldiers, guns pointed, ready to shoot whoever ran out.

Just then a Congolese Major drove up in a Jeep, ran out, grabbed Dr Williams and hurled him into the Jeep. As he drove off in front of his astonished men, the Major turned to Dr Williams and said, "That was close! You were almost killed!"

Later Dr Williams found a piece of paper in his pocket with a verse from the Bible. It read: "They will lay no hand on you, no harm will come upon you." His commending church in Dublin, Ireland, had given him the verse when they had sent him out as a missionary to Africa.

Told by Jeff Speichinger, Chavuma, Zambia

Finders Keepers

"Did you know there's a car under the sand?" the Kamba chief asked my father as we prepared to cross the wide, sandy Kaiti River on our way to Nzaui, where my father was building a memorial chapel in honour of Peter Cameron Scott, founder of Africa Inland Mission (AIM) who had died there in 1896. As a ten-year-old, father had taken me along to help with the brick making.

"How do you know there's a car under the sand?" my father, Gordon Stephenson, an AIM missionary, asked.

The chief told the story. About two years before a medical doctor had been touring the area. He tried to cross the Kaiti River but got stuck in the sand about half way across. A storm in the highlands sent a torrent of water rushing down the river before they dug the car out. The water swept over the car, burying it under the sand.

"Do you know where, exactly?" my father asked.

"Right here!" the chief said, pointing.

Father noted the spot. He later asked the District Commissioner what laws applied to a car that had been left under the sand for two years. The DC said if the vehicle had been left over two weeks with no one watching over it, it was considered abandoned and whoever dug it out could keep it.

Before we made our next building trip to Nzaui, father packed all the tackle he needed to raise the buried car. We drove down the mountain from Mbooni, the mission station where we lived at the time, to Kivani on the road to Kilungu and came to the Kaiti River crossing where we camped. The chief called everyone to help and hundreds of people showed up. Using *kerais*, wide but shallow metal bowls, they dug out the sand. Soon a lake formed around the car as water seeped into the hold. Eventually the top of a boxbody car appeared.

Father floated a dried-out fig tree bole over the roof of the car and then tied a rope to it and around the bottom of the car. He attached a rope to the front and everyone pulled the vehicle out. It was a Chrysler Durant. Father checked the oil sump and the differential and neither had any water leakage or damage. Father drained the oil in the sump and put in fresh oil. He also changed the gearbox differential oil, cleaned and dried the various bits under the bonnet and installed a new battery. He inserted new spark plugs and cleaned out the petrol tank and the Durant fired up. He used the Durant for his mission work for the next few years before selling it and buying a Ford Model A boxbody for £15.

John 'Steve' Stephenson, Nairobi

When I Get to Heaven

Sometime in the mid 20th century, a visitor from the mission office in London visited Kapsabet and gladly consented to preach at the Sunday morning church service. Jean Baxter, one of the missionaries working at Kapsabet, was asked to interpret his message into the Nandi language. The visitor started rather dramatically, wanting the congregation to know he looked forward to meeting them in heaven one day. We wondered how Jean would handle his flowery opening sentence, "*When I plant my feet upon the shores of eternity...*" Without batting an eye Jean rendered this brief but accurate translation "*Ye aitu Kipsingwet...*" (When I get to heaven...) Doubtless the listeners wondered why the Englishman had to take so long to say such a short phrase!

Jack Pienaar, Cape Town

Dad's Black Bicycle

Back in 1946 in Tanganyika my dad didn't have a car, but he was responsible to visit various villages miles away. My father, who was known as 'Hap,' travelled on his bicycle. I can still picture my father ready to leave on one of his missionary safaris, a 50-mile ride to a village called Butundwe, among the Sukuma people. Across the mid-support piece of the bike he carried his .22 rifle in case of any trouble from wild animals. On the back fender dad carried his humble blanket, his 'bed' when he slept on the dusty dry mud floor of an African house. He'd share his resting place with four-legged residents such as calves and lambs, which were kept inside at night for protection from predators. Chickens with chicks also bunked down in the warmth of a cosy corner.

On the front of Dad's two-tired transport was a large light to show the way as he pedalled to his destination. Batteries were hard to come by, but this clever light was pedal-powered, providing light on the path when daylight faded.

My father carried very little food, relying on the kind hospitality of the local peoples he went to visit. He knew how to travel light. Dad always travelled with one or two African Christians with whom he had built close relationships, as he was their Bible schoolteacher.

A bicycle didn't offer much protection from the sudden thunderstorms or dust devils sweeping across the expansive plain, which would later be part of the Serengeti National Park.

Being a white person always drew curious children who hovered around Dad looking with intrigue and interest at this funny pale man with strange clothing and wearing a pith helmet. He used the opportunity to befriend the children, showing them this bleached bwana meant no harm.

Dad pedalled so far on his bike, took risks, slept on dirt floors, ate African food, patched punctures, crossed swollen rivers and exposed himself to strange diseases to pass on his faith and make disciples in Jesus' name!

Elaine Barnett, Florida

Hazards of Government Officials

Mrs Rainbow Assaults DC with Wastebasket

Mrs Rainbow of Nanyuki became so annoyed with Clarence Buxton, the District Commissioner (DC), over some long-forgotten disagreement that she grabbed the nearest wastepaper basket and jammed it on Buxton's head.

Unwilling to accept this insult to his leadership, Buxton charged Mrs Rainbow with assaulting a government officer. The punishment for her action was a fine or a period of time in jail. Mrs Rainbow refused to pay the fine, insisting she be jailed instead.

Aghast at the thought of her friend in jail, Mrs Rainbow's neighbour came to the office and offered to pay the fine on her behalf. Mrs Rainbow refused the help and demanded to be jailed.

This created a dilemma because Buxton had no proper place to incarcerate a European woman. He finally solved his problem by sending Mrs Rainbow to Mombasa where she was jailed in the old prison in Fort Jesus to serve out her (presumably short) sentence.

Tim Hutchinson, Gilgil

Hunter Shifts Border

A defiant old hunter, who had freely roamed East Africa for years before there were any hunting restrictions, resented any interference with his shooting. After Britain and Germany had divided the Sultan of Zanzibar's possessions between them, he went hunting near Kilimanjaro and was confronted by large signboards marking the new political border – DEUTSCH-OSTAFRIKA German East Africa. As most of the game appeared to be behind this line, the hunter spent some time moving the signs back about ten miles. He enjoyed a very rewarding time shooting and claimed to have "added a sizeable chunk to the British Empire single-handedly."

From Jennifer Stutchbury's unpublished manuscript, **Time's Eye**

Retrieve My Teeth, Please!

After the First World War I was invited to join the Kenya Administrative Service as an Assistant District Commissioner (ADC) as District Officers (DOs) were called in those days, and posted to Eldoret in 1919. I reported to my District Commissioner (DC), an elderly gentleman named Mr 'S' who had previous service in Bechuanaland. He told me since I was very young I wouldn't be much of a companion for him as he was rather fond of his liquor. Once I rescued him from drowning in his soup when I dined with him. He had overbalanced with his face in the soup plate and was struggling to recover. On another occasion he arrived at the office with only one gum boot. I pointed it out and he said he had stuck in the mud while walking to the office and must have withdrawn his foot and left his boot. Would I recover it please?

Another time he arrived without his false teeth and his speech was almost unintelligible. He related that the evening before he had had a rather thick night at the Pioneer Hotel and had retired to the long drop to vomit and unfortunately his denture had gone down the pit! Would I arrange to recover it? A gang of prisoners was summoned from the gaol, one lowered on a rope, and the next morning my master's speech was understandable again!

K L Hunter, condensed from mini-SITREP, published by the Kenya Regiment Association of KwaZulu-Natal

Unprepared

I showed up to the office of the Ministry of Works in Nairobi at about 10 am after dropping various labourers off to their worksites. My supervisor looked at me in surprise. "Why are you here? Go to Government House right away!"

Assuming there must be some electrical job to do, I set off still wearing my short trousers. I walked into Government

House and saw a line of blokes from the Ministry of Works (MOW) wearing ties in the ballroom. Governor Baring and his wife had called all of us up to make a special presentation as a thank you for our work. They gave each of us a framed photo of themselves as a memento for our services. Somehow everyone else had been forewarned and had dressed up for the occasion. I received my gift wearing my short trousers!

Dick Whittingham, Langata

DC Golfs Across the Desert

Long ago the District Commissioner (DC) in Lodwar enjoyed his remote bachelor posting so much he refused to take his annual leave. Finally authorities sent him clear instructions he had to take his vacation.

The DC left Lodwar with his golf clubs, one hundred golf balls, a small gang of porters and some enthusiastic Kenyan children to find and retrieve lost balls. He drove golf balls across the sandy wastes and over lava flows all the way to Lake Baringo. He had taken his leave, he'd satisfied the authorities and he could now return to Lodwar.

Anthony Dyer, Nanyuki

Prison Meals

My father, Reg Ward, ran the Manor Hotel in Mombasa for a few months while the current manager and his wife took a much-needed rest. While he was there a prison van used to call in every day to collect the meals for one of the European prisoners held in Fort Jesus. Apparently it was usual for the Mombasa Club to provide the food but, in this particular case, the cad had been blackballed from the Club and so they refused to supply the food!

Rosalind Balcon

The Royal Standard

During the Queen Mother's visit to Kenya in the late 1950s they flew the Royal Standard from the flagpole at the entrance to Government House. One day the person in charge of raising the flag made the mistake of putting two ends of the rope through the grommets on the Royal Standard instead of a joined loop. That evening when they lowered the flag the entire rope came off! I received a call after dark asking if I could repair the damage. I drove to Government House, where I often worked on the electricity and lighting, with an African worker from the Ministry of Works. He shinnied up the flagpole and threaded the rope through the pulley. The Royal Standard flew the next morning!

Dick Whittingham, Langata

Prison Blankets

In the Trans Mara area of Maasai there was a local jail holding short-term prisoners for local petty crimes. Security did not need to be tight. One prisoner had permission to visit the local *dukas*. Later he had to be charged with theft of prison blankets, which were found on sale at the *dukas*.

Robert Mathews

Helpful Advice?

In 1906 Randall Swift and Ernest Rutherford, the earliest European settlers at Punda Milia in Makuyu, tried to plant sisal but when the cash crop did not do well, they sought the advice from the director of agriculture in Nairobi 50 miles away. Here is his reply: "Well where you are at Punda Milia you are rather too high to do any good with fibres and you are too low to grow wheat or barley. Of course maize and beans would do well with you, but then you are too far from the market. Then there is stock

– that should do well, but really there are so many diseases in this country that I would not recommend that. In fact Punda Milia is one of those betwixt and between places, and I am glad I did not advise you to take up land there."

Submitted by Muigai K Harrison, Njoro

Trout at Archer's Post

When an Indian trader from Isiolo decided to try his luck catching catfish in the Ewaso Nyiro River at Archer's Post he hooked a large trout, presumably trying to swim from a mountain stream on Mount Kenya to the ocean. Never having seen such a fish, the man took his catch to the DC at Archer's Post, who informed him he had caught a trout. Frowning the DC asked, "Do you have a trout licence? You can't catch trout in Kenya without a trout license." The man admitted he didn't have a trout license. Sensing a nice fish dinner coming up, the DC said, "You can get into a lot of trouble, you know, catching a trout without a license." The man began to sweat. "I really should fine you," the DC went on, "but since you didn't catch it intentionally and you came yourself to bring the evidence, I'll let you go without a fine." The man breathed more easily. "However," the DC concluded, "I will have to confiscate the trout."

John Vaughan, Naivasha

Mounted Kenya Police Explore Cave

Later on in the Emergency my brother Robert and John Chart were together running a section in the Rift Valley. One morning they were on patrol on horseback in the badlands near Eburru where they came upon a cave. They decided to investigate. They handed their horses to their accompanying askaris and went in on foot, side by side. The cave was absolutely pitch dark and neither of them had a torch. They continued slowly until suddenly there was the most terrific noise, something coming at them at speed from within the cave. They had no time to unholster their guns, or to retreat. The colossal noise came straight at them. They simply stood their ground. A large warthog charged out from the dark recesses of the cave, passing right between them. The two very shaken men and the askaris had a lot to talk and laugh about.

Francis Foster, Tiwi, Kenya

DAO climbs Kijegge Mountain

Coffee was grown under strict colonial regulations in some parts of Kenya but not in Meru until Senior Chief Gideon Mwirichia was permitted to start growing coffee in Meru. Our District Agriculture Officer (DAO) was short, rotund and sweated a lot. He was the only authority enabled to inspect and licence new sites for growing coffee. His idea of 'work' was to commute to his office in his 4WD Land Rover wagon and return home in the evenings.

I was the District Assistant (DA) at Nkubu on the infamous road to Embu with its 99 hairpins in 99 miles. Nkubu was a lovely small administrative centre 15 miles from Meru and went from the forest line of Mount Kenya down to the 2000 foot level of the Tana River. My District Officer (DO) was Peter Leyden, an expatriate. Kijegge mountain rises to 4800 feet almost on the Tana and in Tharaka area. My wife Margery and I had climbed Kijegge several times. It was difficult because of the 'wait a bit thorns' and rocks but the view of the Tana and northwest Kenya surpassed anything we had seen.

Our DO had a wicked sense of humour and started a rumour that coffee was being illegally grown on Kijegge. The DAO was incensed with anger and eventually had to visit and see for himself. He arranged to meet us at Nkubu, but we were occupied 'elsewhere' in the location and left two guides to show him the way.

To reach Kijegge you drove 18 miles to Mitunguu, then 30 miles to Marimanti, then 11 more miles on a very bad road to Chiokarige from whence you walked an hour to the foot of Kijegge. The DAO eventually made it to be met by Senior Chief Muguika at Chiokarige and started off. Many hours later an exhausted DAO made the top of Kijegge. He hadn't found anyone growing coffee. Rumour has it he had to stay resting in bed when he finally got home. Peter Layden and I laughed over it all for a week!

Peter Barnes, Naivasha

Kifaru!

I was a District Officer in Marsabit from 1953 to 1955. We always travelled with askaris because of the danger from Ethiopian bandits and wild animals. One night while on safari I was wakened by shouts: "Kifaru, Kifaru!" (Swahili for rhinoceros.) I leapt up in one movement and crouched behind my camp bed, rifle in my hands. Actually this rifle was more something to hold onto than an effective weapon against two tons of rhino; it was only a .22, suitable for shooting birds, and I would probably have achieved more by using it to hit the rhino over the head than by shooting at it. I could not see the rhino, but could hear it thundering towards us as it made its first charge. I also heard an infernal racket as pots, pans, tyre levers and other available metal ware were banged together. I joined the others shouting and yelling. The rhino veered off, clearly not quite sure what it had come up against. A few minutes later the rhino charged again from a different direction. Upon being greeted in similar fashion it decided it might have better luck elsewhere.

David Nicoll-Griffith, York, U.K.

Outhouses

Do Not Disturb!

A left turn off the pathway from our veranda passed between tall parallel kei-apple hedges. A little further on the hedges widened to enclose a sheltered spot. In the centre, facing east, the structure coyly referred to in that era as "The Little House" stood resplendent.

Indoor facilities had not yet reached Tambach, the remote administrative centre where, between 1949 and 1953, my father, John Raymer, served as Principal of the Government secondary school and teacher training college. This classic upcountry long-drop toilet (with the inevitable yellowing bound copies of the *Daily Mirror* hanging from a nail in the wall) was a pleasant place in the morning with the sun streaming through the open door and a colourful flower bed opposite to contemplate. Footsteps could be heard from afar, allowing the user ample time to warn anyone approaching that the little house was already occupied.

My father retired daily to this haven after breakfast before departing to conduct morning assembly. House rules and the tyranny of the timetable dictated that he be undisturbed during his occupancy of the little house.

On the morning of February 6, 1952, I dawdled over a slice of toast at the breakfast table. Father was we-know-where and Mother was in the kitchen seeing to the day's meals, when a vehicle pulled up sharply at the front gate in a cloud of dust. I ran outside to investigate this unusual occurrence. The Police OCS leapt from his official Land Rover. "I've just heard on the Police radio that the King died last night," he said breathlessly. (In those days of rather primitive technology, radio reception halfway down the Kerio Escarpment was so poor that nobody else in Tambach kept a radio set).

Rising to the occasion, I promised to tell my parents this shattering news. Surely, I thought, such important news must merit a slight relaxation of normal household rules? As the OCS drove off, my small legs carried me swiftly past the veranda and left up the kei-apple walk, ignoring the warning sounds up ahead. I rounded the corner. There, enthroned in the morning sunlight, sat my father, colonial khaki shorts at half-mast. "Daddy, Daddy!" I gasped, the bearer of momentous news. "The King's dead!"

"B----- off at once!" he snarled.

Dee Raymer, Machakos

Exploding Loo

My friend Alec, the neighboring DO in Meru District, had a problem with his choo. Bluebottle flies emerged in angry hordes whenever the lid was lifted.

Alec had an answer to this. In his particular armoury were a number of old anti-personnel phosphorus grenades. If he pulled the pin and dropped one of these grenades down the choo, surely it would blast all the flies to bluebottle heaven?

Dressed only in shorts and gym shoes Alec entered his choo, pulled the pin out of the grenade above the seat and dropped it into the void. But the grenade fired immediately. His bare body, legs and face were spattered with burning phosphorus and he was blown back out of the choo door onto the ground outside.

The Sergeant of Tribal Police and Alec's *mpishi* (cook) heard the explosion and rushed to his aid with water. Alec was sufficiently aware mentally to prevent them pouring water over him, which would have worsened the damage to him. Instead they rolled him in the sand and in a blanket to extinguish the worst flames. He was propped up, spreadeagled, in his official Land Rover and driven within twenty minutes to the nearby Consolata Hospital. He was still smouldering on arrival.

For 48 hours Alec was too ill to be moved. After that he was flown by air ambulance to the (then) European Hospital in Nairobi. His injuries were horrifying; he had burning phosphorous splashes to his bare legs and to his bare chest and the inside open palm of the hand, which dropped the grenade, as well as to his face. The corner of his mouth and his eyelids had taken the blast. It's amazing he survived as a phosphorus grenade is designed to kill.

The medics did a wonderful series of operations to restore Alec and he also received generous support from the government department, which employed us. After six months of treatment he was invalided home, as an almost new man, and restored to civilian life.

Neil McGlashan, Tasmania

Snake in the Loo

When my grandparents died in 1957, we moved to live at their farm in Thika. Soon after the First World War, my grandfather had built the large and spacious farmhouse of mud and wattle, on stilts and with a *mabati* roof. Although the house was plumbed, the plumbing was not connected to any storage, so a tractor brought water in drums from the dam every morning.

The loo was a long drop situated in a large stand of bamboo not far from the house. Early one morning my mother came back from this secluded spot and announced that there must have been a big wind in the night as there were twigs all over the path to the loo and on its seat. When my father went to investigate why there were only twigs on the path and not on the lawn, he discovered my mother had been stepping over and then sitting next to a new hatching of baby puff adders.

Later in the day he went to the loo and we soon heard him let out an alarming roar. We saw Dad flying down the path onto the lawn with his pants round his ankles, shouting he had been bitten by a snake. On inspection he did, indeed, have two puncture wounds on his bum. We scrambled to find out what kind of snake it was so the appropriate antivenin could be administered (we all kept these in our drug cupboards and, when they expired, they could be returned to the chemist who would replace them).

Someone grabbed a torch and we all trekked to the loo to peer down to see the snake. We spotted a pair of shiny eyes and there, sitting on a ledge, was a very angry broody hen who had objected to her view being blocked and had given Dad a hearty nip!

Val Corr (nee Frost), Naivasha

Privies I Have Known

On the farm the 'privy' was always a long drop, down a path at the back of the house - the polite name was then 'the little house.' Coming back with my sister after dark, she'd shout, "Snakes and crocodiles!" and we'd race back as though the devil himself was at our heels, our sturdy hurricane lamp swinging at our side.

My father had his own long drop behind the posho shed. The whole edifice had a slight list and into its depths were reputed to have rolled innumerable torches, as well as cousin Rowley's gold pocket watch.

Down the road lived an elderly couple called the Hampsons. They lived in a little wooden cottage with a real cottage garden. At the side of their house was a large and rather grand long-drop named 'the picture palace,' as Mrs Hampson had stuck pictures cut from magazines all around the walls. We kids loved it and would all crowd in and take turns looking at all the pictures.

When my parents moved to their small ranch near Mt Kenya, they had an indoor flush toilet installed for the first time, as well as a telephone, albeit a party line! But my father still preferred his outside long drop, which perched on a slight incline overlooking the river which ran through their garden. Here he could read his rain-spattered Blackwoods magazines and listen to the river rippling by.

The least savoury long drops were often found at coast houses. These harboured horrors like large spiders in the cracks in the walls, and one day a snake dropped from the makuti roof onto my mother's head! Luckily she was wearing her wide-brimmed straw hat, and the snake, probably as surprised as she was, dropped to the floor and slithered away through a gap under the door.

Margery Barnes, Naivasha

Haraka

Haraka, haraka, haina baraka, says the Swahili proverb. Hurry, hurry has no blessing. A district Officer had a dwelling on a bluff overlooking a river and two *choos* (or to be more correct, *vyoo viwili*). One was near his house, convenient and nicknamed "Hurry." The other outhouse commanded a large view, restful, and so earned the name "Baraka."

Robert Mathews

Target Practice

Many years ago, on an estate called by the locals 'Baba Ndogo's' near Ruaraka, lived a family I once knew. The house was one of those lovely old colonial bungalows – built on stilts with a veranda running round three sides. The only drawback was the toilet. This was a long-drop at the end of the back garden. The lady of the house, being rather house-proud, had planted flowers around this small building and had a heart carved out on the upper half of the door.

The master of the house, being frugal, started to complain that the toilet paper was going too fast! The boys stoutly denied 'overuse' of the loo paper! But the disappearing Bronco continued to cause a problem.

One sunny Saturday afternoon the Old Man decided to clean his revolver. His older son sat beside him, watching with interest. With the weapon clean, oiled and reassembled, he loaded it. "Where's your mother, son?"

A quick look. "She's in the kitchen, busy."

"And your brother?"

"In his room reading."

"Right," the Old Man said. He sighted the gun, took aim at the loo and pulled the trigger.

At that, the door of the loo burst open and out flew a very frightened African youth with his pants around his knees as he bolted for the fence, on the other side of which was the White Rose Drycleaners depot.

The lady of the house arrived hot foot crying out, "We're being attacked! I heard a gunshot!" Father and son sat there open-mouthed, watching a black posterior, rather hobbled by the White Rose overalls at half-mast, disappearing over the fence.

Honour was restored when there were still boxes of Bronco stocked in the long-drop at the end of the month.

S. O'C.

Rough Medical Care

Where Would You Tie the Tourniquet?

My grandfather Dr Kenneth Doig was the local doctor in the Nyeri, Nanyuki area, from 1924-1946 when he retired. He would have nothing to do with cars and so my father, Alec Doig, usually acted as his chauffeur.

One time my father was driving him to see a patient in Nanyuki. They had the usual puncture and grandfather went and sat on the grassy bank while father fixed the puncture. After a very short while, grandfather felt the ground moving under him so he stood up and found he'd been sitting on a puff adder. The snake quietly moved away!

Grandfather's made only one remark to my father: "Alec, where would you have tied a tourniquet if it had bitten me in the bottom?!"

David Doig, ex-Nyeri

Bwana Daktari Makes Painful Mistake

Shortly after the Emergency, my father Brian Shaw of Kipkebe in Sotik, took on a new farm Dispenser, a very forceful character known to all as Henry. We decided to send him on a six-week medical course to Kaplong Mission. After completing the course, Henry returned imbued with even more confidence in his medical ability and soon became widely known as the "Bwana Daktari."

I was filling in as the farm assistant to my father, and happened to be in the dispensary when a rather woeful figure appeared, complaining his left cheek was swollen and "*umaed sana.*" Henry confidently told the patient he had a bad tooth in the left upper jaw. In went the pliers. Out came the tooth.

The unfortunate sufferer returned the next day, his cheek slightly more distended. Henry regretted he had made *makosa kidogo.* The bad tooth was located in the bottom jaw. In went the pliers. Out came the tooth.

When the poor man returned the next day, obviously in some distress, with a very swollen cheek, I felt the time had come to intervene. So I told Henry that without wishing to question his medical knowledge or diminish his medical standing in any way, the time had come to send the unfortunate man to Kaplong for a second opinion.

He returned later that evening, looking really ill, with a note from the Doctor, which read as follows: "This man must be quarantined at once. He has mumps."

The patient recovered in due course (without losing any more teeth) and Henry's standing as the Bwana Daktari remained unimpaired.

Michael Shaw, Limuru

Friendly Witch Doctor?

I was the junior DO in Handeni District in 1960 in Tanganyika. Handeni, in Tanga Province, was a dry, underdeveloped district bordering Maasailand and had a long-time reputation for the practice of witchcraft or *uchawi* in Swahili.

One day the court clerk came to me and said, "Sir, we have a lunatic outside. What shall we do with him?" I immediately referred the matter to my DC, Geoff Bullock, and we pored over legal notices for the correct procedure to follow. It turned out the man was a respected schoolteacher who had apparently been bewitched. The poor fellow was now babbling incoherently and frothing at the mouth. The DC arranged for a medical examination, but no illness was diagnosed. He was committed to a mental institute and sadly died within two weeks.

My district messenger, Rajabu, said to me, "There is nothing you Europeans can do, Bwana. The witchdoctor has put a curse on him."

The next month a delegation of witchdoctors arrived at the

Boma and asked to see the DC. They wanted to be formally registered as a Friendly Society under the Friendly Societies Ordinance. Eventually the case was sent to the registrar of Friendly Societies in Dar es Salaam. The application was turned down.

Professor Edgar Hibbert

Missing Finger

Farmer's wives in old times kept a useful medicine cupboard for treating the family and farm workers. This might comprise Epsom salts, iodine, homemade bandages, eucalyptus oil, cough mixture, quinine, embrocation and the indispensable aspirin tablets. Also M and B, tablets and powder, which acted as a great antibiotic.

One day in the 1950s two men appeared at our back door for treatment. They were strangers who had come out of the forest with a rather wild appearance and we thought they might be Mau Mau. A strange hush fell on the farm as workers repaired to their houses in fear and dread. News always travelled fast. The cook, who summoned my mother, could hardly conceal his trembling. My mother calmly collected her first aid box and went out to see what had to be done. One man had a missing finger and his whole hand was swollen. My mother duly cleaned the man's hand with disinfectant, liberally covered it with M and B powder, and carefully bandaged him up. The men were then served mugs of hot sweet tea with plenty of aspirins for the wounded one. The men disappeared as mysteriously as they had come.

My mother always claimed that her kindness to the man with the missing finger was the reason our farm was never attacked.

Margery Barnes, Naivasha

The Leopard Cure

Dr John Gilks kept a tame leopard, which he took with

him when visiting patients. It was called "Starpit." The Africans thought that was its name as they heard Dr Gilks reprimanding the leopard, "Stop it, stop it." One of Dr Gilk's patients who was ill in bed with a liver complaint claims she was cured by sheer fright when the leopard came in behind the doctor and leapt straight on top of her in bed.

*Suzanne Fisher, from **We lived on the Verandah***

Save That Leg!

It was Aunt Daisy, or Gran Griffin as we all used to call her, who saved my left leg from being amputated. I had scratched it on something and it went really, really rotten. The doctor said it had to come off. "No way," said Aunt Daisy. She then scraped my leg clean. She put a rubber sheet on the bed, then cotton wool then gauze on my leg. She poured half-a-gallon of cod liver oil all over it and did this for two weeks. I recovered and today I don't even have a scar on my left leg.

Shayne Perry, UK

Witch Doctor Power

It is easy for the sceptical to discredit the power of witch doctors but I witnessed their power. We had a man in Nairobi who would arrive each morning for work, make straight for the curb just inside the entrance to the factory and remain there, head in hands, all day. He would return to his quarters at the end of the day.

When questioned he claimed a witch doctor had set a curse upon him and he would die. He said someone banged heavily on his door every night and was driving him mad. Enquiries from his colleagues who lived in the same compound revealed that none had heard any such banging.

I visited the quarters at Pumwani, Nairobi. They formed a

hollow square and there could be no doubt that if there was any banging, all around would have heard it. At the suggestion of the company doctor, a psychologist/psychiatrist was called in. After a number of consultations, he declared he could do nothing for the poor chap. He thought perhaps a period at his home might do the trick but, on his return from compassionate leave, nothing had changed. Within days the man was dead.

Dick Corner, South Africa

Sleeping Off a Spell

Doctor Vonnie Petrie worked in Nakuru during the late 1920s and the 1930s. My husband, her eldest son, tells the following story: One day one of Dr Petrie's workers came with a major problem. A witch doctor had put a spell on him and he was due to die on Friday that week. The man was grey with fear and trembling. What was the answer to this problem?

Dr Petrie had the answer. She gave the patient an anaesthetic, which put the man to sleep for twenty-four hours. When the man awoke it wasn't Friday because Friday had passed. It was Saturday and so the witch doctor's spell had not succeeded in killing the man!

Sue Petrie, UK

Bowing to the Sultan in Zanzibar

When I was the Chief Medical Officer in Zanzibar in the late 1950s, we had to be alert when a red limousine drove by as it was the Sultan of Zanzibar going for a ride. If you found the red car in front of you, you had to slow down and patiently drive along behind because no one was allowed to pass the Sultan. And if the Sultan was coming towards you, it was customary to stop your car by the side of the road and get out and bow.

One day I had a doctor friend visiting from Chattanooga,

Tennessee in the US. We went for a drive on the island and I spotted the Sultan's red car coming. We pulled to the side of the road and I informed the visiting American doctor on how to bow slightly to the Sultan who gave us a royal wave as he went by. As we got back into our car the American doctor chuckled and said in his southern drawl, "If the folks back home knew I'd just bowed to a coloured man, I'd get lynched!"

Told by Dr Bill Barton, Nairobi

Buffalo Shoots Hunters

Two African men came into a medical clinic in northeast Congo to be treated for some nasty wounds. As the missionary doctor stitched them up, he asked them what had happened. "Oh, a buffalo shot us," the men explained. Curious, the doctor pressed them for the rest of the story. The men had gone out hunting buffalo with an old-fashioned muzzleloader rifle, which they had loaded with rusty nails and other bits of sharp metal. The two men had stalked the buffalo and when they got close enough they aimed and pulled the trigger. The hammer clicked loudly, but the rifle failed to fire. The buffalo heard the click and turned and charged. The two men dropped the muzzleloader and scrambled up a nearby tree for safety. The frustrated buffalo attacked the rifle with its horns and somehow flipped it in the air where it suddenly fired – and shot the two hunters up in the tree!

Steve McMillan, Kijabe, Kenya

My Wife's OK, But...

I was born in Uganda near Jinja many years ago. My father had notified the nearby missionary doctor to attend my mother when the birth pangs arrived. However, the doctor was detained and my father ended up delivering me himself. Once I had been safely born, my father decided to use our pet baboon baby to tease the tardy doctor. Father had the baboon dressed in swaddling clothes. When the doctor finally arrived, my father met him and informed him the baby had already been born. "Zoe's fine," my father said with a straight face. "But I'm not so sure about the baby," he continued, handing the baby baboon to the good doctor who received quite a shock. The doctor and my father had a good laugh and remained good friends for many years.

Frances Foster, Tiwi

Long Train Ride

While we were in Mombasa for Easter weekend in 1974 a Goan boy was hit by a safari rally service car in Nakuru. He was admitted under the care of the late Dr D'Cunha at the Rift Valley Hospital with a fractured thighbone. Subsequently he developed 'Fat embolus' and threw a bit of fat from his fractured bone into his brain and became unconscious.

Having heard me at a surgical conference reading a paper on how I had successfully treated two cases of this unusual complication at the Aga Khan Hospital, D'Cunha traced me in Mombasa through that hospital. I advised him to fly the patient to Nairobi and I would return to Nairobi by the overnight train and take over. In the meantime I instructed my team to start our standard management.

My family and I caught the train on Easter Sunday and reached Voi in time. Having been stationary there for a long time and seeing a lot of commotion on the platform, I went to the station-master to inquire. Apparently the goods train, which preceded us, had knocked an elephant, which had strayed from Tsavo onto the railway track. The dead elephant was lying on the railway line blocking both trains. There was no telling when the line would be clear for our train to move.

I knew that D' Cunha's patient had been admitted under my

care and my team was waiting for me. I decided to walk into Voi town and hitch a lift to Nairobi. Having unsuccessfully waited for half an hour, I walked to the petrol station where a lorry driver who had stopped to fill up took pity on me and asked me to jump on the pile of hessian bags in the back of his lorry. Happily he was in a safari mood and landed me at the hospital in four hours flat. The story has a happy ending because the patient did well and is now a practising lawyer in Nairobi!

Dr Yusuf Kodwavwala, Nairobi (More popularly known as Yusuf Dawood by his newspaper readers)

The Doctor is Out - at the Cinema!

Liberty Cinema, the first cinema in the Pangani area, opened sometime in 1958. A very popular Indian doctor had his clinic right next to the Liberty Cinema. The small waiting room was always crammed with patients. But that never deterred the doctor from taking ample breaks to enjoy a few scenes of the film being screened next door, before returning back to the waiting and the ailing. Very often his first question to his patients was if they had seen the latest Indian film and whether they had enjoyed it. He would even recite dialogues, criticize the actors and heroines or confirm the wordings of a particular song. He gave the same antidote to all his patients – little packets with the same white pills, wrapped in newspaper! The doctor is no more, his clinic long gone, but some of his ex-patients still swear by him and the efficiency of this style of treatment!

Neera Kapur-Dromson, Nairobi

Sports and Games

Rough Golf, Naivasha 1908

Time was when the march of events in a British territory, in course of development, was marked by the successive appearance in the locality of first the missionary, then the trader and the soldier; and when the man of war gave place to the tax collector the settlement was complete. That was before golf absorbed all the leisure (and in some offices a part of the "working hours") of most officials, for now no district can be regarded as properly developed if a golf course is lacking...Naivasha has a course, but, down to the date of the preparation of this volume, the history of its Golf Club was a blank sheet, for no club had been formed, and the course was made and was maintained by private individuals. "Colonel Bogey" has therefore still to pay his official visit to the links, and the records are yet unwritten, although a correspondent, to whom application was made for information about the course, says that he once did the first hole in 2, but he modestly adds that this was a "curious mistake" rather than a "record."

The golfer who cannot do without the velvet turn and smooth lawns of an East Anglian summer course would probably turn up his nose at the sport provided by the Naivasha course. It occupies a few acres of the quarantine area, and possesses no buildings except those made by ant bears, and it is impossible to illustrate this account, because all the players have strongly objected to being photographed on the course in its present condition.

From 1908-1909 British East African annual

Wrong Venue

As the members of the Kenya Harlequin rugby club from Nairobi battled the road to Mombasa in a convoy of private vehicles on their way to a fixture at Mombasa Sports Club, high above them in an airplane the Mombasa rugby players were flying to Nairobi. Both clubs arrived at the other's field to find no team to play against. The fogs of time have obscured which fixtures secretary got the venue wrong, but it's likely the one from Quins endured much more scorn and abuse for subjecting his team to a futile 1000 kilometre bum-numbing road trip.

From ***The Book of Rugby Disasters and Bizarre Records***

Nairobi's First Golf Course

There remains Nairobi, the principal course in the country, on which the championship is now annually decided. It owed its conception to the energy of the late Mr Bell, who formed the club and laid out the original course in 1907. Naturally it has been gradually improved from year to year, and its present excellence is undoubtedly due to the great care and perseverance of the present secretary, Mr A E Gardner. It must be confessed that the course represents, as in most African courses, the triumph of the game over natural obstacles. The soil is mostly clay and the grass somewhat sparse and rank; but, as elsewhere, regular play is rapidly improving it, and as year after year it is fed down by sheep the turf gets shorter, crisper, and thicker. The greens are of sand-covered earth, very true but naturally forming a very difficult space on which to remain. (There can be no question here as to the merits of run-up or pitch.) It is hoped gradually to replace them by grass. Nothing could be finer than the situation. A bird's-eye view of the town is obtained on one side and the Ngong forest skirts the other, while on a clear day Kilimanjaro to the southwest and Kenya to the east reveal their snow-clad peaks. It gives an added thrill to the visitor to know that both lion and leopard still haunt the Ngong forest. Within the last two years an officer in the Kings African Rifles came on a party of lions, and was badly mauled, if not, as is usually stated, actually on the course, little more than a long drive distant. There are a few snakes in the long grass and "rough" bounding the course. These form an extra incentive to keeping straight!

Lord Cranworth in his 1912 book, ***A Colony in the Making***

Rugby Cures Wart

My friend Louis Zanos was built like a square block and with his amazing speed, he scored most of the tries for our school rugby team at Rift Valley Academy. He also had a troublesome wart on his knee, large and ugly. No treatment could get rid of the wart. One evening after a rugby game in Nairobi, our school bus was wending its way down the escarpment road back to our school at Kijabe. Suddenly Louis shouted out from the seat behind me. "It's gone! My wart! It's gone!" We turned to have a look and sure enough there was a small crater on his knee and the wart was gone. On either side of the place where Louis' wart had been were neat teeth marks. His wart had been bitten off, probably at the bottom of a loose scrum!

Shel Arensen, Old Africa Editor

Presidential Pig Hunt

My Grandmother's first home as a married woman was at the Government Experimental Farm at Naivasha, where my Grandfather, J K Hill, was the Manager with the title of Assistant Director of Agriculture. VIPs often visited including on one occasion former US President Theodore Roosevelt and his son Kermit.

My Grandmother writes: "Round the Naivasha District, and indeed, in many parts of Kenya, warthog abounded. Part of the Farm experimental work included very valuable imported boars and sows. The wild members of the pig family carried 'Swine Fever' a disease lethal to imported stock so we were at pains to control them. Pig sticking was started, but owing to the large number of ant bear holes it proved too dangerous for horses and riders. We therefore, organised periodic 'pig drives' and shot them. Theodore and Kermit expressed a wish to help us and so one evening after tea, we started off to beat up a nullah, a favourite place for warthog.

"Full instructions were given to the four beaters that on no account was any of them to go ahead of the guns and all four must keep in line. We impressed this upon them and asked if they understood, to which they replied, "Ndiyo Bwana.' My husband and I took one bank of the nullah whilst the Roosevelts took the other. We had worked along slowly without any result and, as the light was beginning to fade, a shape bearing what looked like very large tusks appeared up ahead in the gloom.

"Shots were fired whereupon three beaters who had been crawling along on all fours in the scrub rose from the cover with debarked Maasai throwing sticks clamped firmly in their teeth! The fourth lay wounded. They carried him to the top of the bank whilst I went home to collect the buggy and pony and returned to the scene. Two of the men drove him to Naivasha to the Indian dresser who patched him up and put him on the next train to Nairobi."

In the gloom with a whitened stick clamped between his teeth as he crawled through the scrub, he looked like a prize tusked warthog! By great good fortune he had not received the full shot, but one eye was badly damaged. He returned to the farm later and went off full of smiles to his reserve taking a very nice cow as compensation!

Fortunately he lived to tell the tale, as did the members of the shooting party who had another extraordinary story of Africa.

Charles Harris, Portugal

Converting Rugby Balls

At halftime during one of the Impala-Nondies rugby matches in which I was playing, I was told my 8-year old son Toffer went onto the pitch and enthralled the crowd by meticulously placing the ball and kicking conversions. After two successes he went for a third attempt and set the ball. At that moment he needed a pee and stepped aside to relieve himself. Finished, he turned to the ball and paced carefully backward for the next kick. The crowd collapsed with laughter, but my son was too engrossed in what he was doing to notice.

Andrew Cobb, Durban

Almost a Hole-in-One

I was golfing with my son at the nine-hole golf course at the Aberdare Country Club. On one of the par three holes, my son Adam hit a wonderful shot. It went straight at the pin and rolled closer and closer to the hole. We got excited, sure he had managed a hole-in-one. But as the ball neared the hole, along came a warthog and picked up the ball!

Pat Scott, Gilgil

One-Armed Bandit in Mombasa

I recall that in the 1950s the Mombasa Golf Club, which celebrated its 100th year in 2011, acquired a 'one-arm bandit' fruit machine as an addition to the club amenities and to supplement the club income, which mainly came from bar takings. The acquisition was well received by the mainly male members. However, R S Campbell (my father), a three-times past Captain and Honourary Life Member, considered that the younger bachelor members – in particular those from the Union Castle Mail Steamship Company's bachelor mess in nearby Cliff Avenue – were spending unaffordable sums of their hard-earned income on the gambling machine. Father had the machine uprooted and unceremoniously deposited in the creek adjacent to the first tee, where it surely lies to this day.

Ian D Campbell, Nairobi, Kenya

Camouflage Disaster

We agreed that for successful hunting in the forest, silence was one of the essential points to be observed. Having got over this trouble by discarding our boots, George decided that khaki was not the ideal colour to blend with the undergrowth in the forest and suggested green as being far more suitable. He therefore sent a boy into Jinja with one rupee and instructions to buy a tin of dye… The boy arrived back with a gaudy looking tin, covered in Indian writing, which was full of very pretty looking green crystals. George immediately emptied about half the contents of the tin into a basin, added lots of water, got all our khaki shirts and trousers and dumped them into the basin. They emerged a beautiful green.

Next day, clad in our lovely green clothes, we went off full of confidence to try and get meat for the pot. Trying to walk about quietly in the shade of the forest may sound to anyone who has not tried it, a most restful occupation but in practice it is quite the reverse. At each step one has to take care to avoid stepping on sticks or dry leaves, or anything else likely to make a noise. And one has constantly to keep stepping high over small shrubs and bushes that would rustle if touched, or else one is bent double trying to dodge branches and overhanging tree trunks. It was particularly hot that day and we therefore had not gone far before we were all sweating profusely. I started to itch and very soon noticed that Fronny was scratching himself too. Then George started. At first we did not take much notice, just put it down to an odd flea or two we had brought with us – there was no shortage of these in the banda – but it soon became obvious that there was some other cause.

We called a halt and I happened to notice that Fronny's neck was a vivid green. I glanced at George's and found his the same. I drew their attention to this and looking a bit closer we could see that green was mixed up with little red blisters. It dawned on us simultaneously that we were all being poisoned. I vaguely remembered having heard in my chemical course at Uckfield that most green dyes were poisonous owning to their arsenical content. All idea of hunting was given up and we beat a rapid retreat to the house where we shouted to the boy for a bath. By this time the little red pimples had developed into big angry looking blisters and we were like a pack of monkeys scratching ourselves. What we did not tell George about his green dye was not worth listening to. However, once we had bathed the irritation did not last long. We all spent a rather uncomfortable night but were more or less cured by morning. The boys spent the next day boiling our clothes and trying to get them to their original colour.

George was still worried about the colour scheme questions and suggested to Fronny and me that we try making a solution with ant-hill earth and putting our clothes in that – the idea being that the buck would mistake us for ant-hills instead of leaves. However, Fronny and I were not very polite about this, and said we would rather do without meat and stick to our diet of sweet potatoes and matoki.

Hugh Foster in the book **Uganda Adventures** *published by his son*
Francis Foster

Me Kenyan!

Remo Pollastri, an Italian former-POW, worked on a farm in Nakuru for Mr Manuel. He played rugby for Nakuru. I still remember his big wide body in a game against my team, Nondescripts from Nairobi. Remo didn't speak English very well, and introduced himself saying, "Me farmer."

In this game he received a pass on the goal line. If he caught it and fell to the ground he would have scored and Nakuru would have won the game. Remo knocked it on. An annoyed Nakuru player yelled at him. "You stupid wop!" (Wop is pejorative word usually used to refer to Italians.)

Remo's immediate reply: "Me not wop. Me Kenyan!"

Irving McLean, Langata

Rugby Players Really Push Up

One weekend we drove in our Standard Vanguard for a game against Eldoret. We hit a rainstorm on the Timboroa hill and got stuck in the mud as we tried to grind up the steep grade. We all got out and put on our rugby boots for better traction and we pushed and shoved with my wife Mary at the wheel. When we finally struggled to the top of the hill, we were exhausted. We made the rest of the journey to Eldoret without incident, but they thrashed us in the game. We were too weary from pushing the car up the hill. Two weeks later Mary told me she had a confession to make. "Do you remember pushing the car up Timboroa Hill?" I nodded. "Well, I didn't have the courage to tell you until now, but when I got to the top of the hill, I found I had the hand brake still on!"

Irving McLean, Langata

Uganda Wears Black

The Kenya rugby team arrived at the pitch in Kampala for a match against Uganda shortly before World War II. They wore white rugby jerseys. When Uganda showed up, they, too, had white shirts. It looked like the match would have to be abandoned until a resourceful lady produced some black dye and a bucket of water. The Ugandan shirts were dipped in the bucket and were still damp when Uganda took the field.

From The Book of Rugby Disasters and Bizarre Records

Bits and Pieces

Maize on the Cob

In 1946 about mid-day on a Monday morning a goods train of some thirty trucks towed by a small wood-burning engine steadily made its way from Nanyuki towards Nairobi. I shared one of the trucks with my precious pony who was happily munching some lucerne hay.

We had competed at Nanyuki all day Sunday in a Pony Club jumping contest and the return journey to Nairobi had started at 6 pm Sunday evening. It had been an action packed competition and although I had been able to find lucerne hay for my pony, I had never had the chance to replenish my own rations. The bread and cheese sandwiches I had set out with on Friday were by now dry and stale but would have to suffice until I had ridden the five miles home from Nairobi Railway Station on Tuesday morning.

We had reached a part of the journey where flourishing fields of maize grew either side of the railway. The train came to a stop next to a field festooned with ripe maize cobs. Looking ahead from my truck I could see the engine driver and the stoker busily throwing logs of wood from the steam engine's fuel bunker down onto the track side, where they then piled them into a substantial heap. The two men then stepped into the maize field and helped themselves to some ripe maize cobs. "Fair exchange is no robbery."

To a hungry teenager about fifteen years old it seemed entirely right that the engine driver and his stoker should have a snack. I can still remember the mouth watering, delicious aroma of roasting corn on the cob which wafted back from the engine as we recommenced our journey. Only in Africa could a mid-day meal smell so good!

Bob Archer, Darlington, UK

The Lady in Blue

Air Commodore Harold Probyn, affectionately known by all

as 'Daddy', was very much a 'son' of the Royal Air Force. After World War 2 he returned to his home in Nyeri and, still keen on flying, built for himself a small aeroplane powered by a Volkswagen engine. Come the year 1981 he achieved the grand age of 90 and was still flying his plane. To commemorate this milestone the Nairobi Flying Club organised a fly-past in which Daddy participated, the event being recorded by the BBC. According to the *Guinness Book of Records* he was then said to be the oldest pilot in the world to hold a valid licence, but by the age of 92 his flying days were over.

In 1991 Daddy reached the age of 100. By now he was residing in the Nanyuki Cottage Hospital, somewhat frail and sometimes forgetful, but, as ever, humble and courteous. The Nairobi Flying Club, together with representatives from the RAF, organized another fly-past, this time at the Mweiga airstrip, near Nyeri. Afterwards he was taken to the Aberdare Country Club where he met many of his old flying friends to whom he gave a lucid and touching speech of thanks.

About this time the Queen and her husband, Prince Philip, were to visit Kenya and the British Embassy arranged for Daddy to be flown from Nanyuki to Jomo Kenyatta International Airport to meet the royal couple. After the official preliminaries, the Queen, wearing a striking blue outfit with matching hat, and her husband, did their 'walkabout.' The first person they talked to was Daddy. He tried hard to get up from his wheelchair but was immediately put at ease by his distinguished interviewers. The Prince recognised the old Royal Flying Corps tie Daddy was wearing, remarking that it dated him. After a few minutes of conversation the royal two moved on and it was then time for Daddy to be flown back to Nanyuki. At the end of a strenuous and eventful day, and as he was being tucked up in bed, he was asked, "Well, Daddy, how was your day?"

"Good," he replied, "good, but just remind me of one

thing. Who was that charming young lady dressed in blue who came to talk with me?"

Dr Peter Nicklin, Naivasha

Nairobi's First Cinema Show

Cherry Kearton, a pioneer photographer, came to Kenya in 1909 with a cinema projector and some natural history films. Nairobi had just recently acquired electricity thanks to Clement Hirtzel and his Nairobi Electric Light Company. Kearton was determined to hold a cinema show, but his projector's arc lamp required a resistance. He asked Pop Binks to assist him. Binks suggested a water choke, but said it would be difficult.

Kearton scoffed at the difficulties. "The show is tonight at the Railway Institute, and it must go on."

Binks found a forty-gallon cask. He then used two wires to suspend two copper plates in acidulated water inside the barrel. The arc lamp burned brightly, delighting Kearton.

Binks warned Kearton that the water choke acted as a heating gadget and sooner or later the water would boil. Kearton ignored the warning. The crowd arrived for the cinema. For twenty minutes the show went well. Then a faint steam rose from the barrel. In another ten minutes the steam formed a dense column, and after half an hour it was impossible to see across the room.

About that time, the screws holding the copper plates corroded through and the two plates touched, blowing all the fuses in that district of Nairobi.

It was time for the interval, and everyone retired to a nearby bar lit with hurricane lamps while Binks fixed the copper plates and replaced the boiling water with cold. They kept the second session shorter, finishing before the water boiled again. Unfortunately, the steam vapour in the room contained a chemical irritant. Kearton, who had to provide a running commentary for the silent films, was adversely affected by the steam, and coughed and sneezed through his part. However, as this was Nairobi's first cinema show, everyone deemed it a great success.

*From H K Binks' book, **African Rainbow***

Power Move

My mother-in-law gave a stifled shriek in the middle of a film at the local cinema in Zanzibar. She wasn't screaming about a frightening scene on the screen. She had just remembered the cake she'd left baking in the oven!

"No problem," her husband, Frederick Barnes, assured her. He was in charge of Zanzibar's power station during the 1930s and early 1940s. He popped out to telephone the power station. He instructed them to switch off the power to all of Zanzibar while his wife hurried home and removed the cake before it burned. When she returned to the cinema, Fred called the power station to restore power and they sat down to enjoy the rest of the film.

Margery Barnes, Naivasha

Ali's Post Office at Kajiado

Before Kajiado got its first official Post Office, Ali, a local shopkeeper, ran the 'Post Office' as well as running the whole town. In his shop he sold bread (Elliots), margarine (Blue Band), cooking fat (Kimbo), biscuits (Barings), and paraffin extracted by a squeaky pump out of a *debe* into a Treetops bottle. There was nothing plastic in his *duka*. Tin basins were *karais* and the favourite enamel mugs were 'fifteens.' Ali measured *posho* out in Kimbos and sold potatoes by the *debe* (though sometimes the sides of the *debe* had been squashed in). All those words seem now a long forgotten language. Ali had the telephone exchange in a corner of the shop. As he had never come to understand that the wires carried his voice, Ali's voice got louder and louder according to the distance of the caller. Calls for the Boma, two miles down the road, brought a voice that resounded round the shop. We got to know every Government officer's business before it reached him. A Nairobi call strained Ali's larynx, but an overseas call almost brought on apoplexy!

Ali's Post Office was a great convenience to us. He waived all costs for putting our notes to local friends or officialdom directly into their boxes. He faithfully peered at the address on our letters. "It's no use sending this letter for the Education Officer in his own box," he would advise us. "The DEO will be in the County council office all this week. If you have a message for the Public Works man he'll be there too. They are planning the repairs and building plans for the school." He always knew where everyone was. He saved us lots of futile trips to the Boma at the other side of town. "Yes, the DC is in. But hurry, he is going to Loitokitok at 11 o'clock."

But once the government built a real Post Office, buying stamps became just that – buying stamps. We missed the entertainment and information we received at Ali's Post Office in his *duka*.

Lorna Eglin, Hermanus, South Africa

The Rarest Thing on the Coast

As a child, our family often spent holidays at the Mnarani Club in Kilifi. One vacation in the 1960s the Club, managed in those days by Monty and Peggy Hayes, organised a scavenger hunt for all of us children. As we raced around collecting things for our list, we pondered one item. We had been asked to bring back "the rarest thing on the East African coast." What should we bring? We had an inspiration. Monty's bald head still had three or four hairs. If we could pull one of those out, surely that would qualify as the rarest thing on the East African coast. Someone managed to sneak up behind Monty and pluck one of his precious few remaining hairs. Monty wasn't too impressed with us, but with his rare strand of hair our team won the scavenger hunt.

Joannah Stutchbury, Nairobi

Bush Etiquette

Several years before we came to Kenya an old family friend was out here hunting elephant. He wasn't related to us, but we children all called him 'uncle.' In actual fact, it was because of what he wrote back about the country that Pop decided to move to what was then British East Africa.

My uncle was camped way out in the bush in Uganda, I think it was, and somehow heard another hunter was in his territory. At that time there were no such things as hunting blocks, of course, but there were gentlemen's agreements among the few hunters not to hunt in another's area.

So my uncle sent a servant over to this man's camp with a note in a cleft stick inviting him to come to dinner a few nights later to discuss the matter. The man arrived at the appointed hour having walked several miles through the bush, following game trails, and wearing full evening dress. He was accompanied by his gun bearer who carried a rifle, lantern – and the hunter's black patent leather shoes. My uncle thought nothing of this – he received his guest wearing full evening dress himself!

told by Donald Ker and recorded by Edie Ker in a self-published booklet called **Around the Campfire**

Bathtime Blues

When I was a young 'sprog' living with my parents in Tanganyika during the Ground Nut Scheme in early 1951 at the age of three I decided to give them great anxiety at the worst possible time. We were being transferred from Hogoro to Kongwa and on moving day we stayed overnight with our good friends the Reillys. Auntie Vera was bathing her daughter Carol and my sister Jane, who were only babies. My mother Mary and Auntie Vera were waiting for the return of my father Leslie and Uncle Gerry from the accounts department at Hogoro. Both girls bathed. When they looked for me and Brian to give us the same treatment, we had disappeared! Panic!

A dirt road led up to the house, which stood on a hill surrounded by bush and plenty of wildlife. It was about 5 pm and would be dark by 7 pm. The neighbours were rallied and both fathers called and an organised search started. Everyone was allotted an area, including the local Wagogo complete with spears and shields. Some of the women stayed behind and prepared sandwiches and drink for those reporting back. As searchers came back without having found us, our mothers became even more anxious. Torches were provided and more people arrived to search.

Somehow Brian and I had managed to dodge in and out of the bush while walking down the track away from the house. We found our way into my father's office. And that's where someone finally found us when they saw the lights on in the office and went in to investigate. I was playing on the typewriter and Brian was sorting through some paperwork. It seems we must have been hiding near the accounts office at the time our fathers rushed home to help in the search.

John Gardner

Train Scare

Early in 1955 I was recruited with many other young Brits by the Crown Agents to go out to Kenya as police to help with the Emergency. We were taken up to the new Police Training School at Kiganjo, where we were accommodated in large tents. During the course, it was decided we should individually take night patrols with askaris to ambush tracks into the forest, which the Mau Mau used to come out to get supplies. My team consisted of nine heavily armed askaris and me with a .45 revolver. We were later dropped off and told to set up an ambush on a well-used path coming out of the forest.

It was a beautiful night with a wonderful moon lighting up Mount Kenya. I soon found a useful place with a large clearing in front and a track going into the bush beyond. Not being able to speak a word of Swahili, I couldn't arrange for askaris to keep watch. In no time we were all asleep. At about 2 am, I awoke to feel the ground shuddering. I saw flashing lights, sparks and noise and assumed we were under attack, so I yelled, "Fire!" We opened up with our automatic weapons, only to see our bullets ricocheting off a massive dinosaur of a steam engine lumbering up a track in the clearing, belching out sparks, steam and smoke amid a flickering fire box.

I've never been so frightened in my life. My team must have assumed I'd seen some Mau Mau creeping up behind the engine. The monster of a train engine chugged on with new holes from our bullets leaking steam as it towed a long line of trucks.

Alan Shearburn, Cape Town

Blurred Vision

I was shooting birds at Kinna at Block 37 with my father and Gulam Hussein Habib. One night Gulam, my father and I drank too much at camp. Father and Gulam decided to sleep in the Land Rover. I woke them up early the next day so we could go hunting. At first father drove. I would point out some birds and tell him to drive that way. Instead he drove in a different direction. This kept happening. I became annoyed and told him to let me drive. I would find some guinea fowl and drive towards them telling father and Gulam to shoot at the birds on the right. They would fire off their guns towards the bush on the left. I stopped the car. "You're both still drunk from last night!" I accused them. Both my father and Gulam denied being drunk. But they decided maybe they should clean their glasses as they both admitted they couldn't see very well. As they took off their glasses to wipe them, they discovered that after their night in the Land Rover together, they had mistakenly exchanged glasses. Neither one could see anything!

Satish Wason, Timau

Tasty Nuts

I arrived in Kenya in 1931 as a young bride to join my then husband who lived in a house just outside Nairobi, near where the Banda School is now. The kitchen was a somewhat lean-to affair and a large tree trunk was used as firewood for the stove. Our first evening meal was eaten by the light of a hurricane lamp and comprised of soup with a number of nuts in it. I dutifully chewed the nuts, which had an unusual flavour. After a while I decided to investigate what they were more closely. To my horror I discovered several dead cockroaches in the bottom of the plate!

by Margaret Wood, one-time owner of Ngong Dairies,
as told by Margaret Downey, Langata

Curious Cow

In 1933 we lived in a house owned by the railway in Tabora, Tanganyika. The kitchen was in a separate small building at the back of the house. A wood stove burned brightly in the kitchen, ready for mother's usual Friday baking session. She needed something from the house and stepped out of the kitchen to get it when to her horror she saw the back end of a cow going into the house! Not sure what to do she stood still. Her imagination ran wild. What was happening inside her house with a cow wandering around? Eventually the cow emerged from the back door, the way she had gone in, and walked to the nearby road. What would my mother find as she entered her home? She followed hoof marks up the passage, left through the door at the end, right on through the living room and then right into the bedroom. There the animal decided to retreat. "Nothing to eat in this place," she must have thought! The cow simply retraced her hoof marks and left the house not having touched a thing on her unusual safari. My thankful mother continued her Friday tasks.

Jessie Durman, Florida, USA

Border Block

Having made one trip to East Africa that ended in Arusha, I decided I wanted to drive from Europe back to Arusha in the early 1960s. Being a bit of an adventurer, I decided I would drive through Libya, Chad and Sudan, something others told me was impossible. It was not an easy trip! I remember arriving at a border crossing between Chad and Sudan. The Chadian authorities let me drive through. But the Sudanese immigration officials demanded my visa, which I didn't have. They told me the only place to get one was in Khartoum. I languished in no-man's land for several weeks, daily pleading with the officials to give me permission to enter Sudan. I couldn't enter without a visa, they told me, but they weren't equipped to issue visas at the border. Finally I offered to use my portable typewriter to write a letter of permission to enter. The immigration officials were tired of me, I guess, because they agreed. I typed up my own entry visa, the officials stamped it heartily and I drove into Sudan and on to East Africa.

told by Hans Shupbach a few months before he passed away in October 2008 in Naivasha, Kenya

Banking in Iringa

The following story - allegedly true – dates from the mid

1930s after the 1929 Wall Street crash and the subsequent worldwide depression. The scene is Iringa in central Tanganyika as it then was. Hot dry and dusty. The banks in East Africa were having a very quiet time. No one had any money and the banks offered no credit. There was no work and not much to eat. The banks, to save overhead costs, agreed to share the services of one travelling inspector. This gentleman arrived unannounced in Iringa one Tuesday morning at about 11 o'clock and went straight in to Barclays Bank. The door was wide open but there was no one inside. No customers and no staff. So the inspector crossed the street and went into the Standard Bank. Again, the door was open, but no customers and no staff.

However, he heard some talk from the manager's office so he went to investigate and peered through the plain glass windowpane in the door. To his surprise he spied the manager of Barclays and his chief accountant and also the manager of the Standard and his accountant sitting playing bridge. The inspector thought to himself "Ah! I'll fix these lazy so-and-sos." He went outside where he had noticed a bright red fire alarm attached to the building. He pulled on the handle and stood back to watch what would happen.

A tremendous clanging erupted from the fire alarm bell and after a short delay a waiter rushed out from the nearby Iringa Hotel with a tray and four bottles of Tusker, which he delivered to the manager's office.

Michael Aronson, Muthaiga

The Wedding Ring

During the 1939-1945 War, Mrs Sylvia Bird was the cheese maker at the Kenya Cooperative Creameries (KCC) Morendat near Naivasha. At the crucial acidity after cutting, the curds are mixed to release the whey. In those days they didn't use sterile, electrically driven stainless steel cutting and mixing machines. Instead, everything was mixed by hand up to one's elbows. One day Sylvia lost her wedding ring while mixing by hand. That batch of curds was packed, matured in the store and sold on the market – with wartime shortages and rationing, they couldn't afford to lose that batch. Sometime later Sylvia's ring was returned to her by a family who discovered the ring in their wedge of mature cheddar cheese.

Sheila Begg, Durban, South Africa

Nappy Duty

While we were stationed in Malindi in 1961 the floods came. We had 16 inches of rain in 36 hours. The house was damp. We only had a *kuni* stove and nowhere to dry the baby's nappies. My husband drove to neighbours' houses with carefully folded wet nappies on a plate to ask them to put them in their electric ovens to dry.

Barbara Watson-Jones, Suffolk, UK

Rooi Piet and the Postmaster

A farmer known as Rooi Piet on account of his flaming red hair used to come to Eldoret town once a month or so on horseback to shop and collect his mail. There were no post boxes. Mail was sorted into cubbyholes and kept behind the counter. I was in town one morning when Rooi Piet rode up and demanded his mail. The Post Master said he should come in and collect it. Piet, still mounted on his horse, rode into the Post Office and attempted to jump the counter. After that, the Post Master would be waiting, mail in hand, as soon as he saw Piet approaching.

L S van Aardt, South Africa

Shilling Mushroom Test

Here is a test for mushrooms taken from *The Kenya Settlers Cookery Book and Household Guide*: With mushrooms one cannot be too careful. Commence peeling the outside white skin of the mushroom, from the edge to the crest. If the skin does not come off easily the mushroom is suspect. To make sure, if not certain, put a shilling in the pan of frying mushrooms. It will turn black if they are of a poisonous variety.

Admiral's End

Trans-Nzoia had a number of military men and quite a few from the Royal Navy including Admiral Crampton, who I'm told captained the King's Yacht at one time. Admiral Crampton had a farm in the Cherangani area and called it Admiral's End. Across the road and close by were Pearson and Warburton who had also been in the navy as midshipmen, who were commonly known as "Snotties." When the sign "Admiral's End" went up our two friends put up their own signboard, which read "Snotties' Bottom." Pressure was brought to bear and the offending sign was removed, but Admiral's End stayed for many years until after the Second World War. I remember going to Admiral Crampton's funeral in the mid-1930s.

John Davies

Fancy Dress

One New Year's Eve many years ago, Muthaiga Club held its usual party and on this occasion guests were asked to come in fancy dress. One such guest, Sushil Guram a Nairobi lawyer and Oxford graduate with a keen sense of humour, decided to go to the dance dressed as a skeleton. This consisted of a black close-fitting outfit with the usual bones and a mask with a skull painted on it all in phosphorescent paint. Sushil got himself dressed up and, wearing the mask as well as the skeleton suit, set off for the Club. However, unknown to Sushil and to all the other guests, the Chief of Traffic Police named Dicky Hoyle decided New Year's Eve was a good time to try to catch drivers who had, perhaps, overindulged and so a number of check points were set up around Nairobi. These were manned by the traffic police in their new uniforms that included a white top to their caps still worn today and universally known as Dicky's little snowdrops. One of these check points was near the entrance to Muthaiga Club.

Sushil came along in his car and two unsuspecting local traffic cops waved him down. Sushil lowered his window and greeted the cops in Swahili. The cops took one look at the skeleton-clothed driver and fled.

Michael Aronson, Nairobi

A Visitor from China

We occasionally had a special visitor in the late 1930s. A Chinaman would show up at our family farm in a van. My mother invited him in each time and he spread his wares out on the sitting-room floor – beautiful and unique things, all the way from China. My mother bought things for all of us, not wanting to disappoint the man. An embroidered tablecloth. Paper parasols for my sister and me. A wooden sword in an elaborately carved and painted wooden sheath for my brother. We treasured these things, and my brother kept his 'sword' for many years.

Margery Barnes, Naivasha

Covered in Grease

We lived on a farm in Kipkarren when I was three to six years old. My brother Fred was a year or so younger than me. One day we discovered a partially empty 44-gallon drum of grease. Fred immediately dived in and began covering himself with grease. I did this more gingerly only covering my face and hands until I saw Fred was fully covered. Not to be outdone I followed suit.

Shortly afterwards my irate father caught us. He said if we wanted to look like Africans we could live among them and began frog-marching us towards the labour camp. While we were not unduly perturbed about going to the camp (as we used to play with the *totos*) what really scared us was the fact that we could be totally abandoned by our family never to see them again.

Next our father beat us with his leather belt and locked us up in the maize store for several hours. After that we were put into the portable metal baths covered with paraffin to be scrubbed down by our servants. I really don't know which part of the ordeal hurt us most. However, the scrubbing was truly painful for several days. I remember the incident as clearly now as if it happened yesterday.

Dave Lichtenstein, Sydney, Australia

Gardener Grows Weed

During World War II we had an Italian Prisoner of War Camp about one mile from our farm at Nyeri Station, now Kiganjo. One day the Commandant came to visit my mother and told her our gardener was selling bhang (marijuana) to the prisoners and could they please look around to see where he was growing it. They duly did and found the beautifully tended weeds growing on the compost heaps! The gardener had to destroy them, there and then. My mother was sure they were just weeds, but didn't allow the gardener to grow any more weeds on the compost heaps.

David Doig, Njombe, Tanzania

Operator Please

I was reared in London and was blessed with the typical cock-eyed Cockney sense of humour. On arrival in Kenya in 1951 I got a job with the Nairobi telephone exchange – the old "spin the handle-operator please" system. Heavy rains hit the country washing away the phone lines to Mombasa. We operators were told to inform the subscribers of the problem and that the delay was indefinite – no radio phones, mobiles or satellite connections in those days. One particularly irate and rude subscriber demanded service so I told him, with typical Cockney humour, that if he got on his bicycle and rode to Mombasa he would get there quicker than any phone call. Needless to say I was politely told to vacate my switchboard and seek employment elsewhere.

Betty Drury, Onverwacht, South Africa

Turn Out the Lights

In the early 1960s the film Born Free was made, starring Bill Travers and Virginia McKenna. The film was headquartered and partly shot on the farm next to my parents' small ranch at Naro Moru using the house that then belonged to Eric and Bettie Sherbrooke Walker. Bill and Virginia Travers brought their children with them to make the film, along with their nanny. I think they all lived in Major Huth's little wooden house nearby. My parents met the Travers several times and found them a most charming and normal couple.

Neighbours were asked to house members of the film crew, and my parents hosted a Mr and Mrs Raines with their son Billy from the USA. Mr Raines was a very tall man and Mrs Raines was a large lady with a very big appetite. My parents privately referred to the family as the long rains, the short rains and the heavy rains! The Raines family did their best to adjust to living on a Kenya farm after an American suburb, but they couldn't get used to having no electricity.

I was staying up on the farm and we had been out for the evening leaving the Raines in charge of the house. On our return later that night we beheld two ghostly figures, father and son, crouched over the two living-room lamps, one an Aladdin that had a fragile wick, and the other a Tilley light which had to be pumped up and produced a loud and persistent hiss. They had gingerly transported the said lights out onto the lawn, because, they said, they were afraid to go to bed and leave them lighted in case of fire, but they didn't know how to turn them out!

Margery Barnes, Naivasha

Ripped Trousers

Tibor Gaal the architect for many hotels on Kenya's beach front, was showing Kenya's first president Mzee Kenyatta a blue print of the house Bamburi Cement was building for him in Bamburi, when a pencil fell from the table. Tibor bent down to pick it up and his trousers tore making a funny ripping sound. Kenyatta looked at Tibor as he stood up and said, "God bless you!"

Andreas Reichmanis, Buechenbeuren, Germany

Nairobi's First Stripper

About the year 1948, Nairobi had one very popular nightclub called the 400 Club that, with new management, changed its name to The Travellers Club. The new manager sought the permission of Michael O'Rourke, the then Commissioner of Police, to employ a professional strip-tease dancer on a short assignment. Michael had a preview of the act and gave his permission on condition that the Club staff should be excluded from the performance.

The show was a great success with full houses almost every night. Eventually, for the final performance by this somewhat overweight lady who was certainly past her prime, she promised to put on a fan dance. There was standing room only for the customers. About midnight, all the staff were sent home and a small low platform about the size of a coffee table was brought onto the stage with a curtain all around it.

The lights dimmed, seductive music was played, the curtains opened and the lady proceeded to dance with a pair of huge ostrich feather fans that hid her attractions from view. At the end of the dance, the lady was back on the platform and then simultaneously she threw the fans apart, the lights went out and the curtains closed. There was tremendous applause and yells of, "Encore, encore!"

Then after a few minutes the lights dimmed again, the seductive music started and the curtains opened. However, instead of the stripper, who should appear with the fans and dressed only in his jockey underpants was none other than the manager of the then National Bank of India (these days called the Kenya Commercial Bank) by name Ollie Mitchell. He too was overweight – in fact very large. But by general consent he was a better dancer than the lady and received even greater applause. Nevertheless, his directors were not amused and the following day Ollie was transferred to manage the new branch of the bank in Bukoba, Tanganyika.

Michael Aronson, Nairobi

You're Supposed to be Dead!

My husband Hugh started his war service with a horse unit, actually they used mules. On the Abyssinian border they were bombed by the Italians. In the mail one day I received a communication from an army official regretting that Hugh had been killed in action on the border. I read it, but did not believe it. Before I had time to take it in and start thinking about a future without Hugh, he arrived on the farm.

"You're supposed to be dead," I told him. "I have a letter

to prove it. I've even received letters of condolence. What happened?" Hugh laughed. It was the kind of joke that appealed to him.

"There must have been a mix-up. There were people killed up there, but I wasn't one of them."

"Thank heaven for that."

Lorna Hindmarsh, taken from her memoir **Beyond Happy Valley**

False Alarm

In 1960 our son William Hutton, aged six, was a pupil at Turi School together with his 'twin' Jane Taylor also of Nandi Hills Tea (both were born the same day and delivered by Dr Ashton in the Eldoret Hospital) and 'Ma' and 'Pa' Lavers looked after them well.

A middle-aged Australian lady named Belita Jardine was the Matron in charge of the boarders at Turi School and was a keen golfer and quite a character.

Well, one evening when she was soaking in a nice hot bath she wondered if she could still whistle by putting two index fingers in her mouth as she used to do in Australia many years before when calling-up dingos to shoot them. To her amazement she found she still had the knack and she was so excited that she repeated the whistle several times. Soon she heard a lot of shouting and the school alarm sirens all went off and announcements came over the loudspeakers. She quickly got dressed and went to the Assembly hall. Armed *askaris* ran every which way and she asked what was going on. She was told that it was believed there were some Mau Mau in the vicinity who had been whistling to each other and it was feared they were going to attack the school. The askaris and a couple of men from the Kenya Police Reserve (KPR), who had been alerted, soon had the situation under control and after a thorough scout around, announced the Mau Mau must have fled back into the bush.

Belita Jardine suddenly realized it was her bathtub 'Dingo Whistles' that had set off the alarm, but she never let on! Those parents 'in the know' had a good laugh and were greatly reassured by the efficiency of the response to the false alarm! Belita Jardine returned to Australia the following year.

Angus Hutton, Australia

Not Worn Winches!

Around independence I worked for a Nairobi car importer. We imported some electric winches as they didn't come as standard equipment with any vehicle at that time. A week after their arriving at Mombasa from their manufacturer WARN INDUSTRIES, we got a memo from East African Railways and Harbours saying they were returning our consignment as it was illegal at that time to import second-hand spare parts for motor vehicles. A month or two of frustrating telephone conversations followed and even the odd telex until we managed to get the message across that the winches in question were not second-hand and even though the description 'Warn Winches' appeared on the invoice, they were most certainly not WORN.

Dick Hedges, Nairobi, Kenya

Safety Precautions

My late father, John Lindsay, chose on a whim to abandon what he considered were rather boring studies at Oxford and came down without graduating. His own father, a highly distinguished member of the Indian Civil Service, was absolutely livid at the time and would have nothing further to do with him.

Undeterred, my father, who was not yet 20, headed to Kenya in 1935 on the British India steamship, the *SS Mantola*, where he stayed with his uncles on farms in Thika and Endebess and saw some of the country. At one point, he was invited to stay with Sir Pyers Mostyn on his farm, Waraza, in Naro Moru near Nanyuki. After a day shooting small game and having retired to the guesthouse after dinner, my father decided to clean his rifle.

Having been taught 'safety precautions' from his early days with an air rifle, my father knew that one should always check that the gun was not loaded and that one should never pull the trigger without deliberately aiming at something. Looking around the room, he opted for the oil lamp on the bedside table. There was an enormous explosion in the close confines of the room coupled with total darkness and a strong smell of kerosene, closely followed by shouts from the main house as his host came running to find out what had happened.

It was regarded as a trivial incident to be laughed at later and lost amongst the many challenges, hardships and great pleasures of farming life in pre-war Kenya.

John Lindsay, Essex

Smelly Carpets

When we moved into a new house in Mombasa in the 1950s, the old lion skins that had covered the floor in our old house became rather smelly in Mombasa's humidity. Mother decided we should buy some Persian carpets from the dhows trading in the old harbour to replace the lion skins. I went with my father. There was much haggling with the dhow captain over a reasonable price for a carpet. On the way home in the car we noticed a foul, fishy odour. It was the carpet, whose smell we had not noticed in the old harbour, what with the general stink of salt fish and the lime-cum-beef-fat used for careening. As soon as we got home we ran the bath, threw in the carpet and soap, and trod the wool like grapes. Before my mother came home from work we had the carpet hung in all its Persian glory on the line in the garden. But for a long time there was a telltale hint of fish in the sitting room.

From C S Nicholls' memoir, **A Kenya Childhood**

Snake Trick

My father, Henry Njite, grew up in the Bunyore area in the 1930s and 40s. One day he and his friends killed a long snake. They decided to tie a rope around the dead snake. They hid in some bushes next to the path that led to the stream where girls often came to fetch water in earthen pots which they balanced on their heads as they walked back home singing and swaying. As the girls approached, the boys pulled the rope so the dead snake appeared to be crossing the path. On seeing the snake, the girls would be scared and run and the pots would fall and break!

Hannington Henry Masiele, Maragoli, Kenya

Eavesdropper

In the late 1940s and early 50s the rural areas of Kenya, if they had phones at all, were served by a party line system. The old phones had a handle. When turned, the phone emitted a ring audible on the other connected phones. Different combinations of four long or short rings alerted the recipient that the call was for them. A single, very long ring contacted the exchange.

I was first exposed to this telephone system when working as an apprentice on our family coffee farms of Kiriga and Githaka in Thika under the manager Major 'Kirki' Kirkland. Our neighbour, Bill Coverdale, who owned and managed Koorali Estate, was a man of great humour.

It was possible for anyone with a phone to listen to the conversation of others simply by lifting up their own receiver. Everyone suspected that one person was regularly listening in, but no one could identify who it was. Bill and a neighbour decided to unearth the eavesdropper. By arrangement, Bill called the neighbour. They waited until they heard the click of someone else's receiver being lifted. Bill then proceeded to tell a corker of a story. At the end his co-conspirator asked, "Where on earth did you hear that tale?"

"Who do you think?" Bill replied. "Old Ma so-and-so, of course!"

"No you didn't! No you didn't!" came a strident shout over both their phones.

It is believed that the old dear, who will remain nameless, never listened in on other people's phone conversations again.

Tony Archer, Langata

Printed in Great Britain
by Amazon